"*Waking Up on the Couch* is the journal of one woman's quest for spiritual awakening, from a childhood connection with the 'invisible world' in the midst of traumatic sexual abuse, to a profound remembering of her true nature decades later. With candor and courage, author Beth Miller walks us through her experiences of tears, terror, rage, dissociation, confusion, the ending of a marriage, cancer surgery, and years of intense analysis. In doing so, she shares dreams, poems, insights, and an emerging willingness to drop pretense and be totally authentic.

In meeting spiritual teacher Jan Frazier, Beth's search for awakening seemed to quicken, revealing that the love and freedom she had longed for had actually been present inside her Self. Perhaps the most engaging part of her story comes as she discovers that awakening to her true nature does not look the way she imagined—with the permanent erasing of all discomfort, pain, anxiety, and disappointment—but rather it is an open embrace of all that arises in being human, and a tender reconnection with the body. As life and circumstance invite her time and again to let go and 'die' into the truth of the moment, she feels the great liberation of 'dying into being,' and living beyond egoic self-centeredness.

Waking Up on the Couch is a deep psychological and spiritual exploration, as well as an inspiring invitation to discover for yourself what the author came to realize: 'Through dying over and over, I am One, and I see there is no end. This moment, and every moment, breathes in and out for eternity.'"

—Dorothy Hunt, Spiritual Teacher
and Director of Moon Mountain Sangha

"This is not a book for the faint of spirit. Beth Miller's *Waking Up on the Couch* is a deeply personal account of the metaphysical, psychological, and the ordinary-daily-life steps in her awakening. Beth writes with a disarming clarity about her inner and outer life, describing the tidal waves that consume her and float her to the surface, again and again. In moments, this book may evoke as much fear as it does hope.

Through her story, she teaches us, or rather reminds us, of truths we all know, and yet forget, chief among them is how the personalities we cultivate to survive our social world paradoxically distance us from our experience of ourselves and that world.

She carefully describes the ropes that keep her bound in relationships—needing the love of others, needing people to be different than they are—and in her inner world—the magical beliefs that all will turn out for the best—and then the disentangling of those ropes, thus replacing a false holding with a real one, and one that lets her self dissolve.

With gentleness and deep respect for all that is human, she attends to the dreams, personal breakdowns, readings, and angels that took her to places of extreme vulnerability and powerful growth. Indeed, central to her story of finding divinity within, are the very *human* beings that guided her path. Watching a program about the journey of a lone polar bear looking for a mate who has stumbled upon the scent of a female, she quotes the program's host: 'It is less tiring to walk in her footsteps.' It may well be less tiring, and more inspiring, to walk in Beth's footsteps.

Wherever readers may be in their own journeys, they are likely to find inspiration from the guiding gems in Beth's."

—DONA TVERSKY

"Beth Miller embodies what she teaches: being open and vulnerable to all that human love presents. In the intimate accounting of her journey to awakening, she bridges the 'two' worlds: the inner and outer, and the visible and invisible. The courage she demonstrates in sharing this journey is both moving and inspiring."

—RAMANA, AUTHOR OF *The 7 Steps to Your Radical Awakening*

"In her memoir, *Waking Up on the Couch*, Beth offers an exquisitely intimate and vulnerable account of the gradual (and sudden) unfolding of her awakening. Punctuated by dreams and poetry, the images she evokes lead us where words cannot, pointing directly at the pure depths of silence from which they emerge. As the work unfolds, one can see the personal 'Beth' thin out and become transparent. It is such a gift to share this journey and recognize the many familiar and unique guideposts, which are so beautifully and vulnerably revealed. The story Beth tells of her death and rebirth is best savored slowly. Like the unfolding of any natural wonder or revelation, it happens in its own good time. This book cannot be rushed or devoured with the mind, each page can instead be planted like a seed, allowing it to bear its fruit, which ripens, reveals its sweetness, and decays to become food for the next revelation close behind. I highly recommend this book for anyone who is a lover of the Truth in all its forms. It is both profoundly personal and utterly divine."

— DR. LOREN ESKENAZI, AUTHOR OF *More Than Skin Deep: Exploring the Real Reasons Why Women Go Under the Knife*

"A traumatic childhood can rob us of an authentic life *and* it can be a portal into awakening into our true nature.

Beth Miller, with great courage, shares her journey of healing from childhood trauma. *Waking up on the Couch* brings us into an intimate encounter with what healing, transformation, and waking up looks like from the inside of trauma.

By looking right into the pain and confusion of 'not belonging' anywhere she, over time, saw through all she was not, devoting herself to the discovery and the embodiment of what we are.

She brings to life how compassion, love, wisdom, and spaciousness can arise from the ashes of depression and dissociation, by going to the edge of the unknown over and over again—and again and again coming into her body anew as a more vibrant, alive human being.

This book invites the reader into the ease and willingness of being at one with everything and anything that arises in life . . . the messiness of strong emotions, powerful feelings, difficult and glorious circumstances, and, especially, each other."

—JULIE BROWN YAU, PH.D., AUTHOR OF (FORTHCOMING) *The Body Awareness Workbook for Trauma: Release Trauma from Your Body, Find Emotional Balance, and Connect with Your Inner Wisdom*

WAKING UP
ON THE COUCH

A Chronicle of Letting Go
Death by Death by Death

BETH MILLER, PH.D.

Epigraph Books
Rhinebeck, New York

ISBN: 978-1-948796-35-4

Library of Congress Control Number: 2018956214

Book design by Colin Rolfe
Cover design by Eva Prieto

Epigraph Books
22 East Market Street, Suite 304
Rhinebeck, NY 12572
(845) 876-4861
www.epigraphps.com

To Those Songs

"Your body is a divine stream
as is your spirit.

When your two great rivers merge, one voice is found
and the earth applauds
in excitement.

Shrines are erected to those songs
the hand and heart have sung
as they served
the world

With a love, a love
We cherish."

St. John of the Cross
Love Poems from God

Contents

Foreword

O VER 2,700 YEARS AGO the ancients knew that whenever we experience separation, whether within ourselves or with an-other—when we believe there are two—we will always experience anxiety and fear (Brihadaranyaka and Chandogya Upanishads).

So why have our five senses and mind been bio-engineered to create separation when it gives rise to so much suffering in our lives? And why do we continue to believe in separation, when science has proven, beyond a shadow of a doubt, that separation is a figment of our imagination—an idea created by our mind—that has been genetically hardwired into our DNA?

For starters, our ability to believe in separation serves us in extraordinary ways. It gives us the ability to form social relationships, build civilizations, and manipulate objects in creative ways so that we can drive cars, operate computers, and fly to the moon and beyond. But this same belief also causes us extraordinary suffering. When we take separation to be the only truth—when we don't experience our underlying interconnected oneness within ourselves, and with everyone and everything around us—we will always experience anxiety and fear—which the ancient Upanishads very eloquently state are the parents of all our misery and suffering. Our one-sided identification with our belief in separation creates inner and outer conflict, and is the underlying cause behind wars and our inability to resolve the social and environmental issues that confront us on the world stage.

Interestingly, until the age of eighteen months, we don't experience separation. Until then, our cognitive facilities have not sufficiently matured to create a notion of separation. But, around eighteen months, the process of myelination—the growth of protein around our nerves cells—is sufficient to enable our brain cells to cognitively formulate a sense of self—an ego-I identity—that is separate. In addition, our mind is wired to identify with the thoughts and sensations that co-arise with our emerging sense of self. To add to this mix, we also have the need, due to our need to survive as a social species, to identify with the belief of separation projected onto us by our parents and society, which they have been conditioned to believe. It's easy to see, then, why we so readily fall into believing that we are separate from everything around us.

I distinctly remember the moment when separation came alive for me. At around eighteen months my sister suddenly appeared in front of me. Sister, walls, windows, door, bed, floor, and ceiling all appeared as separate objects before my eyes, whereas a moment before I knew none of these as objects separate from myself. A moment before I wasn't capable of recognizing separate objects. The next moment, my nervous system had become sufficiently myelinated to cognitively formulate separation. One moment, oneness. The next moment, separation.

When I look back, I realize this was the moment when anxiety and fear were introduced into my life. Before, there was simply sensation, without the cognitive ability to discriminate one thing from another. In the next moment, my brain was capable of naming things: sister, wall, bed, window, door, etc. Along with this ability arrived the realization that each object could cause me pain (i.e., my sister biting my finger, which she did from time to time) or pleasure (i.e., my sister offering me a cola, which she also did from time to time).

Along the way, thank goodness, I came to appreciate that while I possess the ability to appreciate the benefits of separation—in spite of its accompanying pitfalls of anxiety, fear, and suffering—I also possessed the ability to experience my interconnectedness with, and non-separation from, everything around me, along with its accompanying benefits of unchanging joy, peace, and well-being. Why? Because non-separateness is a part of my—and your—intrinsic nature as a human being.

While knowing our non-separateness—and its benefits—may be intellectually appealing, until we actually experience it, we will continue to suffer. Why? Because anxiety, fear, and suffering are messengers that our body sends us, to let us know that we are separating; either within ourselves, or from others around us. They're letting us know that we're losing our interconnectedness within, and without. Anxiety and fear are allies. When we attempt to suppress or escape them, their voices grow louder, as a way of getting our attention. The good news is that there is a simple—but not easy—solution to ending psychological anxiety, fear, and suffering. The way out is to simply recognize, welcome, listen to, and respond—not react—to what we are experiencing. As the poet Rumi beautifully states, "Keep looking at the bandaged place. That's where the light enters. Anxiety, fear, and suffering, they are all messengers, sent from beyond, to bring us back home to ourselves."

But welcoming is not easy. Trauma overwhelms our nervous system. It literally tears us apart, both within ourselves, and from those around us. In working with people who have deeply suffered trauma—through birth, accident, illness, physical and psychological abuse, human trafficking, war, natural disaster, and vicarious trauma that comes when we work with survivors of abuse—I've witnessed the internal consequences and ravages that trauma brings to our body and mind.

Welcoming is not easy. Beth attests to this fact, as she shares her heart-wrenching journey through trauma, with all its devastating aftermath. I am grateful to Beth's courage in offering us a window into how to deal with trauma—through all the trials, challenges, and physical and psychological lows that inevitably come—as she learns to welcome and respond—rather than react—to her hurt, wounding, and feelings of separation.

Beth offers us hope. Even more, she offers us faith and trust that come when we're truly willing to welcome all our messengers of anxiety and fear that accompany trauma—messengers that

Beth came to understand were calling her back home to herself—to healing all her feelings of inner and outer separation.

While many of us will, thankfully, never endure the kind of trauma Beth had to endure, we have all suffered the trauma that comes from falling into the belief of separation. This is an underlying perspective that Beth offers us. We have all fallen into the dream of believing we're separate—and have suffered the consequences. This is a journey each of us is conditioned to take, as a consequence of our being human. Fortunately, as Beth beautifully attests, awakening from this dream is also our birthright.

I'm tremendously grateful to know Beth, to know the journey she's lived, and to know her on this side of her life, where she's living in the qualities of unchanging peace, joy, and well-being that she's awakened to. Beth's life is a testament to what each of us is being invited to live: to be fully awake from the dream of separation.

Beth shows us that we can celebrate our uniqueness as separate individuals—with all the challenges and wonders that being human bring to our lives. She also shows us that we can learn to celebrate our interconnected oneness with one another—and the entire cosmos. Beth's journey reveals pain as inevitable, but suffering as optional. Anxiety and fear are messengers calling us back home to health, healing, and our awakening from the dream of separation. Beth's life beautifully demonstrates that when we're willing to turn into our suffering, amidst all of its changing aspects of anxiety and fear, we can awaken to the unchanging joy, peace, and well-being that is always present within ourselves, that can never be hurt or harmed, that's always patiently waiting for us. Beth did. I did. We both know that you can, too.

So, thank you Beth for taking time to share your journey. It's a journey we are all on: to awaken to what we truly are—interconnected, not separate—alive with joy, well-being, and the peace that passeth all understanding.

RICHARD MILLER
PRESIDENT, iREST INSTITUTE
SAN RAFAEL, CA

INTRODUCTION

"Live without thought of dying,
For dying is not truth."

ST. CATHERINE OF SIENA
Love Poems for God

Y OU ARE NOT WHO you think you are.
This book is my testimony of service to the sacred questions of human existence: Who am I and what is my true nature? Where have I come from and what is death? What or who dies? This is my telling of a life devoted to that quest and its knowing. I invite you to the search and the opening into this for yourself. It is a deeply intimate and personal journey, paradoxically completely universal, and it just might bring you peace and joy. It might even end your suffering.

Do not let the details of my personal journey deter you from your own deep knowing. This book is meant as a guide for you, a pointer to what is the deepest truth inside you—the deepest essence of who and what we really are.

Having known from an early age that I was here to evolve, to wake up, and to deepen into fully realized consciousness of the human condition, I offer to you that you also already have what you need to open your eyes to your own true nature. You are already living the life you are suited for, and with a deep acceptance of that you can rest in how it is for you and how it is opening, from moment to moment.

Be conscious of your life. Pay attention to yourself. Notice, with gentle kindness, how you move in the world, and keep your eyes peeled for the layer upon layer of your inner being. There's gold in those hills, the hills of your innermost being—you are a being of love, full peace lies in your depths, in everyone. For real!

It has taken me a lifetime to come out from hiding and its illusions, and to openly live from this true nature. And every corner, fork, and seeming detour led me to here, where I have always been—even in the midst of profound confusion and feeling lost. And from this perspective all the detours and confusion look perfect, just as nature is perfect. It is perfect. The sweet perfection of what is.

Perfect in its unguardedness, nature is undefended. It shows up no matter what. We humans are, in essence, the same thing—tender, open, and unbounded energy. Unpeel and surrender your layers of apparent "protection" and allow the flow of who you really are to have the final say. It's the truth of the matter anyway, whether you are aware or not.

For those of you on the path of self-discovery, nothing need be, or will be left unseen. You can be an open book, nothing needing to be hidden or ashamed of. All can and will be transparent. You are entering a devotion of "unlearning." Being willing to see with fresh eyes—yes, even, and maybe especially, what you were taught to hate or be ashamed of—you will know the power and reward of healing, of transformation, of authenticity, of wholeness. You will experience healing from a state of illusion; waking up to the madness and insanity of illusory fragmentation that has left you feeling separate, on your own, and out of whack. Look inside to where you know that to be true, recognize that "off-ness" and keep looking.

It can crack you wide open. Waking to the essence of what you truly are. Opened wide, free, and abiding in pure rest and joy.

PART ONE:
Die Before You Die

"Ironic, but one of the most intimate acts
of our body is
death.
So beautiful appeared my death – knowing who then I would kiss,
I died a thousand times before I died.
"Die before you die," said the Prophet
Muhammad.
Have wings that feared ever
touched the Sun?
I was born when all I once
feared – I could
love."

RABIA
Love Poems from God

You are not who you think you are.
We are enormously blessed to be able to know what we truly are.
Don't miss it . . . die before you die so you may freely live.

THE WOW FACTOR

I walk down the streets of the city and an old-fashioned garage, wooden doors, opening vertically, tiny and compact, catches my eye. I stop walking and stand there watching as a woman pulls her modern car into the garage, moving carefully and slowly.

I spontaneously say "wow" out loud.

The sky, the trees, the newly sprung flowers, the man walking straight into me, not aware of where he is walking, the rubble of the school being torn down, the wind pushing my hair off my forehead . . . wow!

I am in direct contact with it all.

I am not experiencing fear or anxiety; I am not pushing back at anything, and I don't really have an opinion or judgment of which of these things I like, which of these things I don't care for, or how something might be better if it were different or is better than something else.

And when I do have an opinion or a tinge of discomfort, it is seen as impartially as anything else.

I am aware of moment after moment of living all life directly . . . no barrier . . .

And being happy. I am content for no reason at all, deeply and solidly content, peacefully so, simply reflecting my natural state of being.

After decades of seeking to make conscious what was deeply known . . . and being off-again, on-again lost in the confusion and limitations of the mind.

THE SEARCH

Many years ago I had a dream:

> *I am asleep*
> *There is movement outside my window*
> *The wind and light in concert*
> > *Begin to dance in my bedroom*
> *The wind moves the furniture, gently but definitively—not earth-shaking to frighten*
> *But enough to awaken*
>
> *The light dances a sparkle on my walls and furniture. Is this the support of the divine?*
> *I wonder in my dream.*

2

I become aware that I am picking up a broadcast in my left ear.
It is a radio program—coarse—I need to be still so the message
can be refined and known to me.

The dream leaves me tingling . . . like something treasured is nearby.

What seems important here, what is helpful to know when looking at a life, at your life, is that we are destined (as we all are) to become transcendent and realized.

We are all born into movement, a symphonic movement of breathing in and out, growing and dying, sleeping and waking. Some of us are aware of this movement and many are actively seeking an abiding ease within this movement, an abiding stillness holding this movement. Our lives are an example of this unique and universal thread of existence.

We are born as pure energy—pulsating through our systems, creative and raw. We are sensation, like the small hairs on the back of our necks open to everything and anything. We are light; we are awareness.

At the moment of birth every one of us begins a conditioning process. As software is programmed to run inside a computer, all of us are patterned and conditioned to see ourselves in certain ways, to behave as we were taught, and to believe, deeply and convincingly, that we are who we were taught to be. We learn how to think about ourselves, we learn how to establish a sense of self (even "pretend" selves), and our learning develops into patterns. We form identities, develop personalities and opinions, make memories, and we relate from these patterns of behavior.

We are conditioned and defined by our families, our surroundings, and our life experiences. This conditioning, who we think we are, deepens and thickens as our lives continue, convincing us, over and over, of its substance.

And we are conditioned and defined by the internal defenses (for protection) we erect as life throws curve balls and lightning. Our defenses, our identities, our beliefs make up a large part of our personalities. Such are the building blocks of what we commonly believe ourselves to be. It has always been like this, for your parents, their parents, and every one of our ancestors.

* * *

In this book I use my own life to show how a personality gets formed; how we come to believe in our small self, how immersed and enchanted we become in our stories, and how it can only be dissatisfying (if and when we are willing to admit being dissatisfied in our lives). I use my life to show the undoing of the personality, the small self, how, through the devotion to surrendering all that is not true, we come to live within presence and love, indeed, we know ourselves to be presence, love, and vibrating, alive emptiness.

I look at my life and personality (in Part Two) through the lens of my personal conditioning. My particular life is one of trauma. For me it was the suffering from trauma that prompted, no, relentlessly demanded that I ask the deeper questions about what in heaven's name this life is all about! From the advantage of hindsight, I can see the building of defense after defense to guard against pain and heartbreak. I can see the fences and walls I built around my tender heart, refusing to be fully here in this world in order to try to protect myself from further hurt. I adopt identities for making my way in the world and having some semblance of purpose. I pile on veil after veil, covering my eyes with fog and confusion, in the name of creating a sense of self that could, and would, belong in this world. I adopt beliefs to fit in with society or rebels, and I work hard, real hard, to master that flimsy attempt at control we all work so hard at. And as I live through trauma, I begin to stand further and further away from my life and from my body.

All the while there is that underlying knowing (awareness) that something much sweeter and truer is at play here.

And then comes the undoing . . .

Having reached the second half of my life (in Part Three), I begin a conscious and more dedicated search for a fully realized life. Through the total commitment of surrender to the discovery of, and the letting go of, whatever is not true, whatever is not real, and whatever is not authentic or living in integrity, I enter the realm of dropping my defenses, one after the other, and seeing through the conditioned personality. All that I have built up over my life is up for reflection, for facing head-on, leading me into the light of full realization, and waking up to my true nature. I allow the opening of my heart further and deeper still. I let go of identification after identification of all that I had put into place to convince myself of being someone, even if that someone was mostly unhappy!

This very process of surrendering defenses, identifications, distancing, and beliefs is the dying process—the dying while we are still alive process. This is the death by death by death that naturally opens us to who and what we truly are.

THE CHRONICLING OF THE DYING PROCESS

My story is written as if it is currently happening. My early years show up here as if there is a separation between "me" and ultimate reality. It appeared to me as two worlds—the world of spirit and the world of matter. It is what it looked like until the full realization of my true nature happened. For the integrity of the chronicling, I have let the false division stand.

The second half is also told in "real" time. It is a chronicle of the dropping away of defenses and identities. It is an intimate and sometimes messy view of holding on and letting go, holding on and letting go.

Waking up is an opening and a beginning, not in any way a destination. The second half chronicles the messiness of bringing to light all that is not unified—during and after awakening.

I know I am in good company when I come face to face with the mistaken belief that everything is rosy and feels good after waking up. The second half, in real time, chronicles this "everything shall be known, brought to the light of day, and embodied." I have long held the image of cleaning house to describe finding, seeing, and feeling repressed and dissociated feelings and experiences. Awakening allows and supports the clearing, the cleaning, and the full integration or embodiment of everything that has been left behind. Wholeness, our innate state, is not a concept, but a living, breathing truth. Nothing is or can be left behind.

PART TWO
A Vessel of Grace

WE ARE ALL DESIGNED as beautiful, intricately carved, and delicate crystal vessels. And yet, when God comes to fill us with light, most of us will break from the intensity and heat—our vessels will not be able to hold.

I have been enamored with this cabalistic legend of the shattered crystal vessel for longer than I had any idea what it meant, for my life or in general. For most of my life I was fervently aware of having given my word that I would not break from the intensity of reality (whatever that meant to me at the time).

It is in retrospect, both from prolonged and deep reflection, and from the years and years of studying our human psychology, that I have come to an appreciation for how and why we suffer so and how the truth of our being is hidden in plain sight—what does not and cannot break!

ARRIVING AND BRIDGING TWO WORLDS

"The verb 'to lose' has its taproot sunk in sorrow;
it is related to the 'lorn' in forlorn. It comes from an
Old English word meaning to perish, which comes from
a still more ancient word meaning to separate
or cut apart."

KATHERINE SCHULTZ

The search, the longing, the knowing in me appeared to show up from the very beginning . . . the deepest question of who and what are we has danced in my soul, playing hide and seek as long as I can remember.

I came into this world, as we all do, as spirit, as consciousness, as emptiness/awareness in form. I came in loving. I came in whole. I came in open and vulnerable, we all do, no matter our temperament, no matter what we bring along with us, no matter our circumstances. I arrived attuned, viscerally, to everything and anything—to everyone and anyone. I sensed, I smelled, I touched, I tasted the physical world—hot, cold, hungry, sleepy, wet, and dry. And I sensed, as it saturated my body, the emotional world—thick, juicy, harsh, smooth. As we all are, I was completely dependent on "grown-ups" for everything I needed to survive and grow. I was physically and psychologically dependent. I was dependent for my very survival.

My experience of being the formless in form, my first trauma, and my first constriction, began before I was born. My mother became pregnant immediately after marrying and my father was drafted into World War II, three months after the wedding. My mother went to the doctor for an abortion and had begun the process when she changed her mind. In my imagination I can recreate these moments and see myself glommed onto the uterine wall, my fingertips dug deep into soft tissue while a gushing red river runs by me with the force of a titanic waterfall. I hang on until the fluid dries and the world is safe to let go. I feel determined to survive and "know" from the very beginning that I will be born into an ambivalent and precarious world—the world, as I would see it, as I was immediately conditioned to see it. The confusion of my mother's early attempt to abort her pregnancy left an indelible mark on my psyche. Coming into this world not being wanted has informed my entire character and personality.

My earliest memory is one of having come into this world in great resistance—the resistance showing up, in my mind (when I was able to form understandings) as a scream of "no". I sensed the limited, the constricted, and the smallness. It can be tossed about. Was the sense one of my spirit sensing how small we make ourselves when we live from our limited mental and physical state? Or was it from the stories we tell about ourselves, from believing in the illusion of being alone in this universe? Was the sense coming from the actual womb I came into? I might never know the actuality of this kind of memory, this scream, but I can tell you I lived with this profound resistance of not wanting to be here for most of my life—going in and out of hating the human condition (hating my condition), and knowing the deeper reality right below the surface.

Not being wanted . . . this began the construction and scaffolding of my first and most compelling human identity—a visceral experience of being unwanted and feeling oppressed, victimized, and deeper still—a "convincing" belief that I did not belong here on earth, and I didn't want to be here. Resistance, the seed of our suffering, showed up from the very beginning. This "threat" both situated and constructed fear and the belief that I was on my own, not connected, and an outsider. In other words, I felt as if I was separate and alone. It appeared that I was terrifyingly separate from both the vast immanent stillness of unity, and the lifeblood of the uterine wall. Welcome little one to your human condition.

And so, began the conditioning process, the process we all succumb to, the process of constricting into a worldview. Many of our world views are unique to our family, our culture, and our country's beliefs, but the constriction we all have in common comes from the profound illusion of feeling disconnected, of fundamentally believing we are separate from others, the world, and nature. Simply by being born here, in this worldly dimension, we are saturated with the belief, the patterning, and the conditioning that we are separate beings, set apart from everyone else, encased in our bodies and mind, and that we are our minds and bodies; and to some degree or other, on our own to navigate our way through life. We are physically separate. We see your body there and mine here. If and when you closely watch an infant grow into being a toddler you will see the child begin to see and experience itself as separate from his or her caregivers. He or she will begin to show a sense of "me." She will point to herself in the mirror, say her name, and increasingly show a sense of self-consciousness. She or he will also begin to see themselves through someone else's eyes and will be defined by those around her. "You are a girl." "You love trucks so much I bet you will become a truck driver." "Look at those eyes, what a lover!" "This one has such a temper; no one is going to love him."

This belief, this sense of self, and this illusion of being someone who is apart from everyone and everything sets in motion fear and lack, a deeply rooted dualistic state of mind. For some of us, those who have experienced trauma, this separation often shows up as a deep sense of feeling alone and unsafe. For others this separation shows up with a sense of being special and unique. However this conditioned perspective of separation shows up though, (and it does show up), it ends with a convincing belief in being apart from others, and ubiquitously operates as an us vs. them mentality, a good vs. bad mentality, an inside vs. outside perspective, a right vs. wrong way of perceiving ourselves and the world.

For many of us, as children, and throughout life, the deeper reality of our oneness pokes through into our consciousness. We don't see superficial differences, we speak to trees, we sense an invisible "world." We remember something truer, and we naturally live as curious, open beings.

For the longest time, as I earlier said, this dance, for me, of believing in separation, of feeling I did not belong, experiencing being born as a profound loss, and hearing the music of the deeper reality, showed up as if I was living in two worlds and feeling compelled to bridge them: a human world and a spiritual world. This was the only way I had of trying to comprehend and understand the conflict I felt, and to try to come to terms with what seemed to be two separate realities that I was experiencing. Being conditioned, as we all are, to believe there is a difference between the two worlds, I "saw" it as a need to marry my two internal realities.

* * *

I don't know when I first heard about angels (messengers or bridges from God), but I am very aware of this knowing, this need to bridge the visible and the invisible world within my psyche. The world of matter and the world of spirit. I have long known I was here on earth to be a healer—to help myself and others heal. As I look back and reflect on my life I can clearly see that, by suffering, I came to know, first hand, the struggle and pain of being human, as we all do! To live fully and well in "both" worlds I needed to be grounded and, like the Velveteen Rabbit, real. Loose in the joints, skin rubbed off, and shabby real! Then I would truly know and love the human experience.

From a relative perspective of the small self, it is easy to see, understand, and respect the trajectory of a life unfolding or evolving consciousness back into wholeness (our innate essence). Having been terribly hurt in childhood I wanted to find some purpose in the suffering: being able to heal when I grew up and being able to help others heal as well. It is also easy to understand wanting to see suffering as noble—so I would know what it meant to be human. From a small-self perspective this is meaningful and is the needed engine for making the most of living here, for experiencing, and making sense of the confusion and heartbreak of how we treat each other and ourselves. It is the resilience of the human spirit. It is the deeper call to awakening.

I carried this identity of being a healer with me the first half of my life. Underlying this interpretation of an identity is the awareness and intelligence of our innate health and well-being.

Now look at the summoning to being grounded and real through the lens of the eternal now, in which we all live (whether we are aware of it or not). Everything is happening here and now. Tap into, be in, and sink into the present moment, at any moment, into presence. It is one! It is whole! In this moment, as one you know human pain, you know love, you know transformation and healing. It is all happening right here, right now. All of us are beckoned and reminded of our realness, the essence of our deepest being as presence.

I was nourished and sustained by a child-like belief in God and by my vivid dream life, which began when I was fairly young. A reoccurring dream that lifted my heart on a regular basis showed me finding a mound of coins under the sofa or chair in my family's living room (which doubled as my bedroom). Concentrating on the light housework I was required to do while my mother worked,

I would be carpet-sweeping the floor and to do a thorough job I would have to reach under the chair or sofa. There, lying prone on the floor, reaching far underneath the sofa I would feel around for the satisfying touch of a handful of coins that I had come to expect. And sure enough I would find them, and each time I took a handful the pile would be replenished. No matter how many coins I took into my hands or put into my pockets they would be instantly replaced. I felt wealthy beyond any human gratification and while I did not have the ability to conceptualize the meaning of the dreams, I did feel an otherworldly presence that was familiar to me. I do not remember becoming aware of knowing where I had come from; I always knew, like the way one knows which mother in a crowded room is yours.

My father and mother were emotionally immature and had no idea how to love themselves or anyone else. I suffered through an early childhood of frequent humiliations, physical beatings, slapping, sexual touch, mistreatments, and lack of respect until I left home for college. I made up my own mantras, "This is not bothering me; this is not having any effect on me." All the while feeling numb and living as if I had little to no connection with my parents.

The most serious violation happened when I was twelve years old when I was beaten, raped, and impregnated by my father. My mother was out for the evening and my father was brooding about something. I unfortunately walked into his bad mood and suffered excruciating and lifetime consequences. On the brink of becoming a woman with all the possibilities of being giddy about boys, nervously talking with my girlfriends about our changing bodies, I was stopped dead in my tracks. The violation, the humiliation, and the secrecy (from the rest of the family and the outside world) affected me in such a way that I closed down emotionally while developing a friendly persona and mask to help me get along in life.

There is a legend from the Gnostics, the mystical realm of Christianity, when Eve is to be raped by the archons (evil spirits on earth). God steps in and removes her soul so only her shell would be affected. It would take me years and years to understand that personally and experience its truth.

This trauma, heaped upon an already frightening and volatile home life, further cinched my not being safe. I further hardened my heart and became even more convinced that the only solution was to live outside my body—about ten inches away. I withdrew, recoiled, and dissociated from my body, my experiences, and the world around me. I shut down and "went away" with this further evidence that I was in danger and very alone. I adopted personas to help me function or relate to the people around me. I sincerely believed these protective masks and costumes were who I was. In fact, I preferred seeing myself as endearing and friendly rather than wounded and helpless. My conclusions appeared completely reasonable and necessary for self-protection. My defenses were smart and creative.

I was aware, even as a child, both of the damage within me, as well as a deeper place that was always intact, connected to something more than this time and place, and quietly hidden. Sometimes this "message" of wellness showed up in dreams, sometimes in a felt sense like a quiet river flowing beneath the turmoil. I do not remember ever saying anything about this to anyone (I think keeping quiet about the invisible world is more common for children than we collectively pay attention to). I do not know how I knew to keep this reality a secret, but I did. I told no one about my deep wellness and even knew enough to remind myself that I would take care of the terrible wounds when I grew up.

"I would take care of the terrible wounds when I grew up." This was a great psychological defense as well as a way of protecting me from unbearable pain and distress. Children cannot feel the full impact of not being unconditionally loved. We would not survive. But the pain is something that stays alive inside, waiting for release, recognition, and tenderness. It is something we can feel and face as adults though. I did intuit correctly.

In retrospect I see the shell that feels and felt damaged, wounded, and injured is a shell and nothing more. Like a seed that is underground, being nourished by the soil and the elements, germinating in the dark, stillness, peace, and presence surrounds, permeates, and holds everything. And this vastness of presence and consciousness that is and was untouched, unharmed, and un-rippled is what I truly am. Is what everything is. From and within this deep and abiding presence anything and everything is felt, seen, known, and evaporated, like a drop of water in the ocean. This presence and awareness is available for our discovery, our recognition, and is pure love.

Throughout childhood and adolescence, as a political prisoner knows to bide her time, staying connected to her beliefs and source while serving time against her will, I lived a daily sentence waiting for a time I could be free. For better or for worse I did not form any strong bonds or attachments to my parents. Without being able to put it into words as a child, I knew my parents' limitations and did not respect them or assume they were right. I knew in a way I could not explain that I would heal and be of service when I became an adult and could experience my childhood from a distance. I identified with any culture or group that sought freedom as sacred, and I thought about freedom a great amount throughout my life. As a child I wanted to be free from my family; as a young adult I yearned for inner peace (freedom from scarred pain). In my more conscious adult time I knew to desire a mindful and deliberate connection to the divine.

My closing heart reinforced my notion of being unlovable and unable to love. It is easy to understand and empathize with our need to close off like this. It is harder to see how this forms a mistaken and clung-to identity and sense of meaning.

* * *

I came to adulthood having held a crude and not integrated bridge between the visible and invisible world. I had a great deal of work to do to make the bridge conscious and useful. It would require a strong vessel that would need to be strong enough for the truth.

Psychologically, the ego, the sense of small self, needs to be developed and constructed before it can be surrendered and dissolved. One of the consequences of being traumatized and not sufficiently attached or unattached to caretakers is not having ample opportunities of knowing yourself very well. As children, we need others, caretakers, to "bring us into being," "to love us into being,"

13

into a real existence. We need mirroring, caring, containing, and reflection to know our true selves. Not having "enough" of that, most of my energy went into surviving, leaving me out of touch with what I really liked, wanted, needed, or thought about things. I felt fragmented and exhausted from relying on the varying masks and false selves I adopted to relate to myself and everyone else. Without a truer sense of self I could not be aware of my thoughts, my feelings, or what triggered me. As an adult this left me overly reliant on outside forces and other people for guidance.

OF BECOMING

As if knowing my fragility, I found dozens of ways to become strong. Again, it is only in looking back that I understand I was preparing myself to live up to a deep and serious promise; at the time I was aware of needing an inner peace that seemed very important and attainable. In psychological terms, I would define this period as strengthening my ego so that I would be stable and firm for future encounters with the unconscious, and with the ineffable.

I married a gentle man who treated me like gold and gave me tremendous room to grow and heal. We had children and a stable life with sufficient resources to enable me to seek and become strong. I find it interesting that as an adult I was inflamed by the need to search for the very knowing I had had naturally as a child. As a child with next-to-no security and nurturing, I was keenly in touch with the invisible world and, through that connection, was kept warm enough. As an adult, having a life of external nourishment, family and friends, tremendous apparent security and love, I felt less connected to the invisible world. My dream of finding endless supplies of coins stopped as soon as I got married. I carried the secret of who I was in a much deeper place and my dream life abated its intensity; instead offering guidance to my daily life.

Intuitively I knew I needed to strengthen my sense of self. I set about establishing it through the roles of a wife, a mother, a friend, and a "loveable" accommodator and pleaser. I was a traditionalist on one day, a rebel on another, and underneath it all, a seeker.

14

I was in the world much more fully now and could do the work that would become necessary to be strong enough to hold both dimensions. Along with diapers, dinner parties, community boards, and vacations with friends I looked for what might be missing. In this search my husband and I spent fourteen years under the guidance of a powerful couple. Harry and Emilia Rathbun devoted their lives to the questions of "Who are we?" and "Where have we come from?" And, "Where are we going?" Harry was a Stanford professor who was well known and beloved for his last-day-of-class lecture on that very subject. They opened my eyes to mystics, intellectuals, poets, and activists. I studied (to name a few) Martin Buber, Carl Jung, Buckminster Fuller, T. S. Eliot, and Arnold Toynbee.

My husband and I did this work within a community of people who were dedicated to a psychological understanding of our nature and a serious undertaking of great minds who had come before us, in their attempts at gleaning the meaning of life. As a community we carried the underlying question of how we could be contributing in universally beneficial ways to this world. To this end we studied the Old Testament as an evolving mythology of humankind's relationship to a greater force and the teachings of Jesus, extracting the archetypal man and his profound contributions from Christianity's ideology and doctrines.

We spent hours and hours studying the inner attitudes of the prophets, the kings, and the man, Jesus. We looked for a practical and moral compass to guide our own inner approaches and ways of being in the world. At this time (early '70s) these were radical and controversial ideas to mainstream society, but made complete sense and harmony to those of us looking for deeper understandings to life. These ideas brought heretofore conventional religion alive, immediate, and immensely useful. What meant the most to me was having a personal relationship to God. I did not need an intermediary or dogma. I knew this to be a truth. As idealistic and possibly unrealistic the goals of this community sound, these fourteen years gave me a foundation for the inner house I was building and set me straight on my path.

Being in this community stirred my deep-seated longing for belonging. I desperately wanted to fit in and find a place here and at the same time I was terrified. To really fit in would likely have unleashed strong, pent-up feelings of alienation. This was an important step for me. I had a taste for being engaged in a wider and more sophisticated world and feeling connected to other people. From the outside it looked, for all apparent purposes that I did indeed fit in with this group of people.

It also gave me the beginning of an intellectual awareness of something larger than my small life and narrow thoughts. Reading philosophers and having group discussions about the meaning of our lives gave me a template for how to think about things, and to use my mind in ways I hadn't known how to do before.

I strengthened my sense of self by seeing myself through the eyes of this family and trying on the multicolored persona of having a purpose in life and therefore having value.

A problem with the community was its cult-like tendencies. It was hierarchal in nature; it was governed from the top down by the people who proved themselves the "most religious" by their public religious decision. This decision showed up through a long list of do's and don'ts (some clear and some more vague). There were religious ways to spend money, go on vacation, show up in meetings (be honest and outspoken), and be a beacon to the world. Those who did not or could not follow the standard of behavior: supposedly modeled on the life of Jesus, but more realistically on the interpretation of his life by the leaders of the community, were confronted in private and public about their lack of commitment to the one true way.

The solid foundation that I did receive, however, came from the study of the teachings of Jesus. I was raised Jewish, with no formal training but a love for the culture and traditions. Having no background with Jesus, I came to these studies with mixed feelings and some apprehension. It felt blasphemous to enter a world that had been forbidden to me, and since I was not sophisticated enough to understand all the reasons why it was forbidden I could not be sure what serious trespasses I would commit. So, it was a great surprise to me when, through a deep stirring within, I requested to be the one to remove Jesus' crown of thorns in a community ritual enacted at a local sanctuary. The ritual, removing the crown of thorns and replacing it with a crown of roses was to symbolize the transformation of wounding into a whole, vital being—a transformation for Jesus and for those of us enacting this ritual.

And so I entered an entirely different field of possible blasphemy! I both identified with this phenomenal man, Jesus, and recognized his true nature, so far evolved. Again, it is by looking back that I see what this ritual meant to me—I was oddly comforted by the Father's betrayal of Jesus. "Why have Thou forsaken me?" he asks from the cross. I did not understand to the depths what this meant to me at the time or how I related, but I had enough of a glimpse to recognize Jesus as a brother as well as being in the presence of someone whose soul and purpose I could not yet comprehend.

HEALING

After many years of study and practice it became clear to me that it was time to walk away from this community of people. I had discovered what I needed to know and my spiritual path was not as a joiner. I had mixed emotions about that; I had the lifetime desire to belong, and throughout my life confused the transcendental yearning for home with an unquenchable thirst for a material place to lay my head (and stay forever). My unconscious, as before through dreams, told me when it was time to leave. I had two dreams: one, the entire religious community was playing Simon Says and I was walking the other way, away from everyone else playing by the rules, and the other showed the leader of the group first lying on the ground, then head elevated by resting on her hand, then sitting, and then standing. No matter what position she was in, I too, was in that position. I knew I had learned all I needed to and it was time to go.

But go where?

Looking back to my time in the community I can see a few things. There appeared to be two strands running through my experience. Since I didn't feel completely comfortable, sufficiently understood, or seen (a virtual impossibility . . . given how fused I was with my conditioned beliefs of not belonging) I felt, in many ways, still like an outsider. I interpreted this to mean I was further oppressed and misunderstood. I felt as if I had missed out on some manual given to everyone else on how to get along well with others, be loved, and liked. I was unaware of my own unhealed/unexamined grief and despair—and unaware that I was projecting it out onto the community and its leaders.

The other potent strand was a taste of the ineffable, my first mature taste of the essence of our true nature. I had my first inkling, my first glimpse of the felt sense of presence and omnipresent love.

On one hand, this time in community and, especially, leaving the community strengthened my conditioned conviction that I did not belong anywhere and further persuaded me that I was not as connected to other people as I longed to be. It can certainly be debated as to how real that disconnect was since I was so conditioned to believe I didn't belong, I doubt I could or would have seen it any differently. And I was as potentially connected as the next person; I simply did not know how to appreciate it, cultivate it, or open to it.

On the other hand, this passing sense of belonging . . . this passing belonging we all do and aspire to (some managing more convincingly than others) is but a flimsy stand-in and does not and cannot come close to approximating the deeper, fully realized connection to all, to wholeness itself. To what we most deeply long for.

My dreams, once again, were the doorway to knowing. It was time to leave another earthly home.

I entered a vacuum and whereas it was spiritually fertile it was immensely difficult psychologically. It was time to face myself; I read a great deal of Carl Jung's work and found comfort and understanding in how my unconscious mind was relating to my conscious one. I had always intuited its importance but now I had the language and comprehension to find further meaning and guidance from my dreams and deeper knowing.

During my time in the community I had met a woman who had a meaningful impact on me. Though we met through mutual friends she seemed to appear from nowhere. She told me she had a message for me: she could "read" me and wanted to tell me what she saw. "You are like harmoniously tinkling bells that are forever being moved by a gentle breeze, and you are a carrier of consciousness—a person who holds the intensity of what needs to be carried forward." My promise to not break under the heat of God's light had been seen by another human being!

The impression this gave me remains with me today and has always felt eternal. I knew exactly what she meant, and I was incalculably relieved to have someone else finally see. It was her recognition that ignited my path to consciousness in a more intentional way. To begin, this acknowledgment played a part in my ability to leave the community; secondly, it grounded my erstwhile intuitive knowledge of who I was, but mostly it gave me the audacity of my convictions—I have not looked back since then.

The voice of truth is timeless . . . the harmony we are, essentially, lives within us, surrounding and saturating everything. I was able to recognize deeper truths when I heard them. And sometimes it takes "an outsider" to reflect our deepest natures to us—it is up to us to pay close and serious attention.

When I left the community, this encounter with external recognition and the readings by Carl Jung shed some light on what was needed next. To be more useful and to have the inner quiet I desired required me to deal with and heal early wounds in order to make room in the unconscious for clearer messages and intents: to be in tune with the tinkling bells and allow them to resonate outwardly. In fact, around this time my dream of finding an endless supply of coins had returned. This time I was outdoors and walked across a square of tar that had been burned and was now cool. At the diagonal corner there was a hole and inside were antique valuable coins. No matter how many coins I took out they were replaced and supplemented.

I had studied enough, and I had been out in the world enough to recognize that if I wished to fully live a conscious life I needed to face my terror of uncertainty and the unknown and say yes to the fulfillment of my intuited destiny to heal and wake up to my essential nature. This was the beginning of my willingness to let go of old ways. As wrenching as I intuited it to be, I could also sense it could soften the edges of built-up defenses and open me to wholeness and compassion.

I went into Jungian analysis. Here was a place where my unconscious would be valued, where intuitive messages would be listened to, and where my wounds would not be pathologized and labeled. It was an intense period, concentrated on cleaning my psychic house, and integrating a great deal of "shadow" material. In Jungian terms, the shadow houses the repressed and unconscious matter that is abhorrent, threatening, and very undesirable to the conscious mind. It could be called a "dark night of the soul" for its bleakness and ugliness. I suffered a serious depression and yet stayed the course facing the dark.

Under the façade of "having it all together," I had always lived with the conditioned and hidden belief that I was ugly, worthless, and deeply flawed. Because I was depressed these feelings bled out. I didn't have the wherewithal to keep them under wraps. The memories of the early years of sexual trauma came to the surface, after being forgotten and "left behind." I was devastated by having to associate this reality with any part of myself and kept saying over and over that I did not want to be identified as such. Something in me knew I was identifying though. I was identified as a victim and being terribly helpless. I cried from the shock and the shame. I cried and moped. I slept a lot. I went through the days like a zombie, seeing the world through a haze. I was incorporating things about myself that had been buried and shameful. Under the loving touch and gaze of my analyst I was able to look and see.

This was a period of time that I came to understand the courage I had and the devotion I would bring to know myself (Know thyself) and know the invisible world, even to the point of almost breaking the vessel.

Well into analysis I had this terrifying dream. Yet I was under the impression that I was awake and this was really happening:

There is an earthquake. I go to the door with my young children. Outside I see colorful flashing lights interspersed with mysterious shadows. With each tremor I wait for the house to fall, holding my breath with fear.

When the quake is over I step outside holding onto my sons. They are soberly attentive and quietly aware of the enormity of this shake-up. It is now around one in the morning and pitch-black outside. I take a deep breath—it is overwhelming, surrealistic, and exquisite at the same time. My neighbors are walking down the street. I call out to them, "Are your homes all right? Are you all right?" They are not overly concerned. Yet everywhere I see destruction, as if the whole earth has been burned.

There is a large barricade in front of my house, reminiscent of the French Revolution. Suddenly my house begins to crumble and fall. My insides go with it. Everything I hold dear is lost. My life, to that point, is gone.

I heard a friend's soothing voice tell me that out of ashes comes so much more. I know this is true, but at this moment, I can only feel the loss and weep.

Several months after this dream, and within a period of three months my mother died, and I left my marriage, by then of twenty-seven years. I was emotionally alone in the world for the first time since my childhood. Leaving my marriage was extremely difficult, for me and for my family. It had been a place of healing, and I lived in a safe and coddled world, the antithesis to my upbringing and relationship to my parents. Now, though I could not fully understand it, my soul was insisting on independence and freedom, and to achieve it I chose to give up all the apparent trappings of security and conventionality.

I found it ironic that I, who had been devoted to freedom, was scared to be out in the world alone. It took me a couple of years to leave. I felt both relieved to be singularly honest about my path, and jinxed that I kept being pushed out and away from places of comfort.

THE BIRTH OF I/THOU

In the outer world I began an odyssey of self-reliance. I learned taxes, making a living, car maintenance, entering parties alone, hours of quiet, and world travel. In the inner terrain, in my continual spiritual search for a deeper relationship to the holy I took a journey into my unconscious by ingesting a hallucinogen. I quietly admitted to the man who would guide me that I was looking for a direct experience of the divine. He told me it would mean letting go. I let go enough to begin the mystic journey that is close to the sacred and brought me face to face with sublime light.

I lay still in a sleeping bag with earphones, listened to beautiful classical music, surrounded myself with mystical icons, kept my eyes closed, and spent twelve hours touring the underworld of my psyche. It was a phenomenal experience, an emotional ride through the highs and lows of what we call history, time, and space. I maintained a gaze as I viewed myself, my Self, and unrelenting, overpowering light and ecstasy. I did not look away when faced with depravity and suffering. I bore witness to the power and perspective of an eternal timelessness that broke down all dualities into a long unending stream, woven and interwoven.

I experienced opposites: light and dark, in and out, yin and yang. There was a repetition of the intertwining of all time, from the ecstasy of the light in different forms to the pain and agonies of six million Jews, Jesus on the cross, birthing the whole human race, over and over. At the core there is no distinction. Ecstasy, rapture, and agony all melt and meld. It is all too enormous to behold or hold. It needs to be broken into strands and we weave our strands into the world as we know it. The light is too radiant and enormous. Aggression, ecstasy, and pain. So many strands of opposites to be strung and woven together. My job. My task. As I do this I am reflecting the all—which is dissolved into oneness. It, and everything, is fathomless—infinite—there is no end or circumference.

I railed at God for forsaking me:
Where was He—six million Jews?
Where was He—Jesus on the cross?
Where was He—the tragedy of my family?
I screamed and howled at God. "Where were you?"

Weaving, weaving, and weaving. Vivid imagery, very different, took courage and stamina to weave all together.

I promised and said yes to God through so many incarnations. I told Him I would not break—I held and held. My vessel did not shatter.

I have said yes to God so many times it has become a matter of fact.

And I know the archetypal betrayal of that promise. I know the betrayal of God. And I know that betrayal doesn't matter. It is part of the whole. It is experienced and let go.

Experience, weave, let go, and know God.

WEAVING

After this experience I began to understand larger perspectives in all aspects of my life. I understood my parents' fallibilities; in fact, I began to have greater understanding of the human condition. I had always been interested in diversity; read whatever I could get my hands on that would delve into different cultures and races. Beginning at this time in my life I started developing the ability to embody this understanding, truly seeing each point of view. This understanding became very concrete; I learned to forgive my father. *I forgave my father.*

I had chosen to professionally work with men who molested children. I was plagued with wanting to understand why and how a grown man could turn to a child out of anger, desire, and/or lust.

I was strongly drawn to healing, including studying to become a psychologist. Healing beckoned me into the lived experience of the fear and torment that I could not have felt or faced when I was fully dependent on my parents, or too little to contain the force of violence. I instinctively knew I was ready to begin the healing. I was strong enough to begin to feel. Living in knots, emotionally and spiritually, distanced me from presence, kept me believing I was living behind bars or in a straight jacket. Freedom called, even though it looked as if I went directly into prison.

As part of an internship, I co-facilitated a group therapy for fifteen men, some who came for treatment voluntarily and most court-ordered. I was the only woman in the group. I was extremely grateful that I was co-facilitating because I sat numb and frozen for several sessions, fighting off nausea and headaches while listening to the men tell their stories. They talked about their childhoods, expressed their emotional and sexual desires and unfulfilled needs, and graphically described their sexual feelings and behaviors with children.

Some of the men were pedophiles, preferring children as their sexual partners; some of the men regressed during bouts of alcohol or stress and turned to children to relieve the tension. One young man, a popular and handsome athlete, felt entitled by a society telling him he was the greatest and could have anything he wanted as long as he played ball well. Another man, disenfranchised from most of mainstream life because of poverty and lack of education befriended and sexually molested a local vagrant child. Some men were predators, stalking and seducing their "prey" for years; others acted impulsively and irrationally. Some liked little girls. Some liked little boys.

Some denied they did anything wrong even in the face of bulky criminal records while others appeared deeply regretful and ashamed of their proclivities.

I had read all the charts before the first session so I knew the scope of the violations. I entered the room with my back straight and my "protection" in place. I had a Ph.D. I was the therapist, I had access to their records and their parole officers; and they were here because they had to be. Even those who had volunteered knew it was only a matter of time until they got caught so it behooved them to show cooperation by getting help. I was armed with the attitude that the men were in the weakened position and I had the power. That is the defense I shrouded myself in order to enter the room and listen to them.

That night I had a dream:

A woman and I find a couple of male intruders in our home. We catch one of the men and together we hang him over a second story landing and fondle his genitals. We have him over the rail—not much he can do about it.

We then have him on the floor and continue to fondle him. He is at first aroused and then becomes very flaccid. When we get him over the rail again I tell him his losing his erection and becoming soft turned me on.

I experience the power and turn-on of the man's impotence. I am amazed and aware of an important recognition of the power dynamic.

24

After years of feeling powerless before my father's needs, I now knew the aphrodisiac of dominance. Feeling powerful over someone less powerful can be stimulating, a turn-on. When I walked into the group I was scared and felt vulnerable, so I armed myself with the external protections of an authority; in the dream the man had been an intruder, another scary situation. I dealt with the fear of weakness by yielding power. I hung him over a rail, taking away his power and disarming the threat. But I took it a step further and molested him. I misused the newfound power. I am amazed and aware of an important recognition of the power dynamic.

I spent several months working with these men who molested children. I got to know each and every one of them personally. I listened deeply to their pain and rage. I left my protection of false power at the doorway and entered the arena as a fellow human being attempting to understand and help. I found the place we were alike, the place of childlike terror and thin-skinned vulnerability. I found the place we were not alike; I chose to become conscious of the power dynamic so I do not act it out and harm another. I chose to embrace my vulnerability, my tenderness, and not, out of considering vulnerability to be a weakness, act it out aggressively on someone else or myself.

There is tremendous power in recognizing and owning our own demons within. To know that we have the capacity to be the devil and saint, to find this awareness, this oneness for ourselves, in ourselves, to accept and embrace this apparent duality and complexity is to know the freedom of being.

Sometime shortly after my time with these men I had a spontaneous vision. I relived the moment my father was raping me. And then, I was my father. And I felt his anguish, his heavy heart, and his complete dissociation from himself, me, and the act.

I never attempted to understand this. But it opened my heart in a way that mystified me.

How easy it is for us to see the hand of grace and its gifts when we are pleased with what we receive or encounter. What about when we feel wounded, slighted, and betrayed? What then? Can we still see the hand of the ineffable? Presence is neutral, and love is unconditional. Acceptance of what is, what already happened is peace.

It Acts Like Love

*"...Could you also kiss the hand that caused
each scar,
for you will not find me until
you do."*

Rabia
Love Poems from God

Humility and Compassion

*"Can true humility and compassion exist in our words and eyes
unless we know we too are capable of
any act?"*

St. Francis of Assisi
Love Poems from God

ROAD TO BEING

The vision quest, this confirmation of the invisible world, this recognition of the place where the devil and the saint are the same, has given me moments of grace as well as implicit directions for leading my life. The challenge left for me was how to integrate this intensity and care into my daily life and being? I began a purposeful prayer life at this time. I kept an open question alive on an everyday basis—what is needed from me now? I attempted to incorporate this attitude into all my ways of living.

This effort opened the door to a lifetime of challenges. There was no great epiphany that transformed me into a selfless human being. I was susceptible to all of my usual petty annoyances, selfishness, hurt feelings, betrayals, and upset when not getting what I wanted. The visceral experience of the light would fade and even be forgotten and hidden at times. I was mostly aware of just being a human and every once in a while I would be reminded of the invisible world that I knew, but could not keep as a primary focus. Yet, I was becoming stronger and more skillful in my life. I grew more sophisticated through travel, reading, and culture, and

26

I discovered that I could now walk in the world as if I belonged there. I knew that healing was possible because I was experiencing it. I knew that people could integrate their inner and outer worlds because I had been able to do just that. I learned that people who feel good about themselves can move very easily in any circle.

But the challenge was how to keep the purpose and intensity of the invisible world in the forefront of my mind while living this potentiated and integrated life. The challenge was how to live, authentically and naturally in this dimension with a sustaining awareness of why I am doing what I am doing, and why I am here.

LEARNING TO SURRENDER

During this time of strengthening and questioning I had felt for many years that I wanted to write a book on resilience. Or perhaps it is more to the point to say the book was insisting on being written. I thought about it, planned it, and jotted down notes and ideas for many years. Any time I attempted to say no to the project I was "told" (strong intuition) it had to be written. One Saturday I spent the day writing before going to a dinner party. When dressing that evening I looked into the mirror and said to myself, "Why are you holding back? What are you not saying as you should be saying?" That evening, at an otherwise typical dinner party of professionals talking about what they did for a living and how they felt about the current politics of the country and world, I heard a message in my head: "Bring the conversation to a spiritual level." As soon as I did, one of the women there, who heretofore had been known for her expert leadership in a well known corporation, told us she was a medium, bringing messages to us on earth from spirits on the other side. The conversation took a detour for a while, but nobody seemed all that interested in what she had to say. As the evening drew to a close, she asked me if I could drive her home. Sitting in my car, in her driveway, she told me she had a message for me from the spirit world: my book was already "written" and would I be willing to give up everything else not completely necessary (the spirit world seems uninterested in full time jobs, making a living, and what energy that requires), and devote that time to putting words to paper. They suggested I light a candle before writing each time and blow it out when finished for that time.

From that moment on, until the book was finished fifteen months later, I did as they suggested. And what I found was the book did seem to almost write itself. I struggled some, but the bulk of the material was waiting inside for me to put words to paper. I spent every spare moment I had writing; every thought and moment spent elsewhere gave me further material for when I sat down to write again. When I finished the book, I felt finished in a way that is hard to describe. It was as if I had always known this book was a body of work that I needed to express. There was a small quiet voice inside whispering over and over until I listened.

Abiding the call to write the book was not the only way I was learning to say yes when asked. Throughout my life I have been given information intuitively. It has always been distinguishable from any other messages or information, like the static of "did I say the wrong thing at the party last night?" Or "am I smart enough to be friends with that person?" This is a knowing that comes from deep within. It is not esoteric or ethereal. It is usually sound advice and/or wisdom that will enhance my growth and ability to relate well with other people. For example, knowing I would take care of early wounds when I grew up and being told to bring the dinner conversation to the spiritual. When I am told what direction of growth is needed for the following year, or when I receive a dream that indicates a prediction of some sort I take it as real as a letter coming in the mail or a message left on the telephone. It has always been as matter of fact to me as knowing what color my eyes are.

What seems important now about this is that without thinking much about it I became practiced in surrendering to the wisdom and knowing arising in my own intuition. I did not have it "checked out" with anyone else, nor have I doubted its veracity or purpose. I have yet to be disappointed by the results of what I have been told to attend to. My ego had grown accustomed to being second in charge and over the years this surrender has been building up a faith in me that I am not alone.

Throughout all this time I was working hard in analysis and this surrender was tested to a severe degree when my analyst moved away. After many years of working together she had become a mentor and guide. I had not had any other relationship like this; being understood on a regular basis as well as held in a secure and wise counsel while I grew into the person I always was. On many levels I no longer needed her in the ways I had before; I was more aware of my world and myself and was living a fuller and more integrated life. But to have her leave felt alarming nonetheless. In losing her, I was losing a mother I had never had; I was losing a mother who guided me extraordinarily into the wider world. I was losing a spiritual guide who, no matter where I trod, appeared to have been there. But before she left I had a dream:

I am in a square, beautifully tended garden. I look up and see a square hole in the blue sky. Ascending to the heavens through this hole is a gigantically large evergreen tree. At its base is a square wooden base. On the base is the queen who is ascending for her marriage to the king. I am enthralled as I watch the ascent and suddenly I am made aware that the queen is my mother. I am touched and thrilled beyond words.

I watch the ascent. I sit down. As I sit, relaxed and content, a huge wedding bouquet is thrown to me through the hole in the sky. My legs are lethargic, it takes great effort and is very slow going to go over to pick up the bouquet. To the right, in the shadows, I see another woman and I know if I don't make quick and serious moves to get to the flowers, she will take them. I move to claim my gift.

I was moved deeply by this affirmation and once again felt supported by my unconscious during a hard time. But even the dream could not hold my distress of missing her at bay. One evening, feeling quite inconsolable, I sat in my darkened living room, crying. I felt a grief I had not allowed myself to feel before; I had not known how to love like this before. I had been too wounded to allow my love to flow. Now I had loved and was grieving losing her. A very large presence made itself known as it sat upon my left shoulder. It was too large for my shoulder and so it basically draped my entire left side. I felt an immense comfort, unlike anything I had experienced before and one that is very difficult to put into words. An angel was visiting me and I was being told I would be okay. Her presence was palpable, familiar, and natural. I was not alone.

Though I continued to miss this dear woman, I was left with something that could not be taken away from me. I had begun to learn how to humanly love. I had always assumed human love was natural; something we did without training or learning. I now know that we can be too wounded to feel love, too closed off to show love, that mature human love can be developed over time, and that it might take considerable effort. Sometimes we need to dedicate ourselves to seeing and loving ourselves, another person, nature, and life itself.

FINDING AND BEING WITH WHAT IS TRUE

In my continual search for what is true I stumbled upon Gnosticism and sought out Buddhism. I could not reconcile the omnipotence of the Judeo-Christian belief of God and the malevolence I saw and experienced. If God was all-powerful how could He or She allow people to suffer so drastically? Gnosticism, the mystical realm of Christianity, included an ineffable darkness in its belief system as well as imputing an equal value to the feminine. I began to study, especially the symbol of Sophia, the Goddess of Wisdom, who being co-creator with God, came to this earth through being misled but chose to stay nonetheless when she, filled with compassion, saw how she could serve here. According to the Gnostics there is always more than anyone can ever see, the ultimate God is unknowable and completely beyond comprehension. Through another "misleading" this earth was formed by a demiurge—a god of imperfection, answering the question of how, if God is omnipotent, we could all be so insane and live in such a cave of blindness. According to the Gnostics, the God of this dimension is incomplete and it is up to us to bring higher consciousness to Him.

This settled something deep inside me. It put in place a great deal of my own experiences, and even more, gave me a context to further explore and understand our human condition and our history together.

I also studied Buddhism. I was attracted to the ideas of impermanence—nothing did stay the same—and the cultivation of detachment as a way of flowing with the changes, some desired and some fought against. I began to reflect on clearing my perceptions so I might see more clearly and embody the awareness of loving and letting go. Being completely present with what is and not holding onto any moment; instead moving on with the flow of time and life.

Much that I write has the flavor of linear happenings and dramatic conclusions. Nothing could be further than the truth. My path towards increasing consciousness was bumpy, difficult, and often times painful. I understand why so few people undertake the journey. And yet, each opening into fuller consciousness gives my life its deepening aliveness.

SACRED GROUND

As the years go by, the external world at times hums, at times falls apart, and I continue living within the open question: What does life need from me? I am rewarded with gratifying work and continual deepening, sometimes through painful digging and moving aside my ego, and sometimes from graceful moments in beautiful concert with the invisible world.

Interestingly, several of these graceful moments have been in the company of others. I had been friends with a group of kind and loving women for over a decade. We got together for fun outings, to support each other's escapades and ventures, to come up against each other's personalities, and to learn how to resolve our conflicts and disagreements with each other. Once a year we would get away for a few days of catch up and quality time. On these outings we often ate cookies laced with marijuana, which gave us tremendous gifts of giggles and fun as we would sit around and play games or talk with each other. Sometimes, though, the substance took us into more serious places. It was during one of these outings that we all journeyed afar: I began to feel unsettled, somewhat dizzy, and laid down on the sofa. I became aware that veils were rising in front of my eyes and with each veil lifted I sunk deeper into myself, becoming more and more aware of an unusual sensation. I was not sure what was happening, but I knew I had a choice in the matter. One of my friends, taking my hand in hers, reminded me of this choice. Was I willing to go in this direction or was I going to stop it? Veil after veil I knew I was going to continue; I felt a sense of refuge in that decision, but knew that I had no idea what might happen.

At this time, we became aware that another one of our friends was feeling unsteady and the women in the group went to administer to her. Sitting by myself I faced a decision: was I going to stay here and possibly feel left alone or was I going to join the others. Involuntarily I sunk into a deep place within and knew I was being called. Earlier in the day, before we took the cookies all of us went on a long walk. The woman who was not feeling well had at that time sent up a prayer of openness and readiness to receive what she needed. I had not known that at the time but was aware now that we were involved in something larger and I needed to get in place.

As if I knew exactly what to do, when in fact I had no idea, I got up, walked across the room, and sat on the floor at her feet so I could look up at her and into her eyes. As she began to look deeply into my eyes I saw the glimmer of recognition and awe reflected in her eyes. I nodded my head, yes. "What you are seeing is true. This is how loved you are."

Knowing at this moment that we were going to go into sacred territory I found myself checking to see if I was being ego driven or could I allow myself to fall into this experience fully. Reassuring myself that I was "clean" I focused completely on my friend. She was looking deeply into my eyes and it was so vividly clear to me that I was being used for her to see herself and know a love she had not known existed before this moment. "I had no idea," she whispered.

I explained to her that I was the messenger here, so she would have an idea. While the other women sat quietly surrounding both of us this dialogue continued as my friend sank deeper into the arms of love. I repeated that this was not me; I was the messenger and she should not confuse the two. During this time I was also given information about the other women in the circle that might be misunderstanding this exchange. I actually "saw" the misunderstanding as one of the women believed the woman going through the experience was falling in love with me; and I saw all of us talking this through and knew it would be fully understood and reconciled.

As I sat there I was enveloped in a state of suspension, nothing external mattering with only this pure moment to be fully present. While my friend was sitting with a look of awe on her face I was filled with the love she was seeing. It was so clear that this was not of me, and so tangible that to this day I can either close my eyes or keenly focus and be able to see and feel this love. For all the times we talk about something being missing in our lives this was a moment where absolutely nothing was missing, nor would it ever be missing. (I was in the midst of the gold coins from my early dreams.) It is complete, it is full, and it needs nothing else. Even though I know I cannot verbally (or any other way) do this justice, the closest I can come is to describe the energy and feeling as love.

As the moment slowly evaporated we sat around in a circle and began to talk about the experience. The other women asked me if the occurrence has cost me anything. I found it an interesting question and yet knew immediately that it had cost me putting aside my ego, the part of me that relates everything around me to me, the part of me that keeps my bearings, the part of me that knows what time it is and when I should eat. While this is a good thing, surrendering the ego so that the invisible world may shine through it also comes with an energetic cost. It was disorienting. But to stay empty and still meant that I, the ego, at this time could not be present. The ego prefers control and orientation, metaphorically it does not like to feel it is not master of its house. Somehow when the need presented itself I knew letting go was necessary even though it was not pleasant from my ego's standpoint.

I also knew I was not finished with this incident. I could see and feel that I was acting as a bridge; that I had agreed to being born as a healer so that I could do my work here, and that I was being used as a messenger. As I sat in the liminal space between the altered experience and being back in matter I could actually "see" the other side and review the moment of agreeing to come to this dimension as a healer. I was being shown what I had intuited; I was being shown the roadmap for the journey I had assumed I was making up as I went along.

As the scene played out in my mind's eye it felt as familiar and real as my grandparent's journey from Europe to America. At the same time, I was greatly reluctant to tell my friends. It would be the first time that I made public my relationship to the spirit world and my singular devotion to that world. But having gone through this experience together I did not have to be concerned with words not doing justice to the felt experience of what I was being shown. It was better communicated through the eyes, where it was seen and witnessed by others and known for its truth.

MESSAGES OF LIGHT AND LOVE FROM THE INVISIBLE WORLD TO THIS WORLD

As I understood living in "two" worlds, bridging the inner and the outer, the visible and the invisible, the one consistency throughout my life was a singular devotion to integrating the threads of both worlds. Automatically and naturally, over and over again I would plumb into darkness, until the light consumed everything that came to the surface. I would find the truth of agony and ecstasy being one and the same, the oneness, no beginning and no circumference from which everything arises.

Sometimes, through dreams, reflections, or interactions with other people I would become aware of deeper insights into the "marriage" of humanity and divinity. This integration, this transcendent view, this oneness is what we all are.

While working with the men who had molested children, I had such a dream, one that shook my sense of self at the time and propelled me into a larger perspective than I had previously not been able to see. I processed the perspective into an essay.

I am including it here to mark the ending of the phase of seeking—it was an important perspective to my life of healing, transformation, and waking up to our true nature.

The dream:

I am sitting on the threshold of a house and a large, somewhat thin, glistening, black naked man is walking outside, across the threshold. I see his back; he is very taut and lean, extremely strong. I watch him walk across the road to a small trench. He pulls on three weeds and begins to plant them. I am struck by the fact that he is planting weeds and knowing it is an indigenous type of ritual or wisdom.

He turns around and I am stunned by the size of his penis. It is gigantic, almost to the ground. It is also sculptured, into three parts, reminding me of a totem pole. His whole body is luminous. As he is turning around I catch my breath and think to myself, "finally, I am going to get a full view." I am also thinking that I don't believe I could have something that large penetrate me. Certainly it would hurt. I realize I have more than met my match.

I go inside the house to a room where there is a young woman. Something gives me the impression that she is my younger sister. It turns out that she is the lover of this man, and I ask her about the physical aspect of making love when he has such a large penis. She is even smaller than I am. She tells me, "Yes, it does hurt a bit, but not that it can't be done." The problem comes with her responding with thrusts. She is limited in that because his penis fills her entire body, she must remain virtually still.

She walks out of the room and I am aware of feeling guilty that I abandoned her at twelve years old.

The dream itself came out of the deepest valley of my psyche. It was archetypal and personal at the same time. It spoke to my powerfully frightening experience of staggering penetration and violation, as well as my chosen defense pattern of becoming numb and staying very, very still. I was finally going to see a full view—a full view of the abuse and a full view of its effects. I had met up with the twelve-year-old I had abandoned and left to hold the experience and the pain. I was ready to face the ordeal, assimilate its full meaning, and the image I held of myself into my life .

There was a numinous quality to the entire dream—a larger than life and deeper than personal experience. The dream offers a relationship between my personal experience and the mystical realm. The man was god-like in his native perfection; natural, unadorned, and glistening. His oversized and elaborate penis resembled man's tribute to the gods—carved out spiritually as recognition of the divine nature of regeneration. My father and the sex act must have appeared to me larger than life itself—a powerful force equal to a face-to-face encounter with the gods. It would take me a long time to realize and accept this paradox—a betrayal and an initiation.

I have had many mystical experiences in my adult life and they do shake me to my core. I find myself wondering if by healing the earlier transgressions I have reaped the benefit of being deeply receptive, willing, and capable of holding God's powerful messages, not breaking the crystal vessel under their weight and intensity, and ready to use the power to wake up. I have observed that I experience mysticism to the same depth I have experienced the pain. The deeper I feel one the deeper I feel the other.

The man is planting three weeds—a paradox in itself. Normally we do not plant weeds; we pull them up and try to get rid of them. I'm told in the dream that this is a wise ritual. Why would he be planting, giving root to an ordinary, pesky, and unpopular product of nature? He is planting the weeds in a trench near the road. There is nothing beautiful or idyllic about the place or the ritual, and yet it is symbolic and important. There were three in my family, my father, my mother, and me. We were ordinary, troubled, and breaking taboos in secret—not very desirable. But as with weeds, our troubles were part of the human-made landscape. And consciousness offered hope and meaning. The despicable transgression and the ordinary lives could be planted and woven into a healthy psyche and a productive life, and transcended into an understanding of the powers of the universe. Weeds are hardy and resilient; they might not be popular, but they are here to stay. In planting them ordinary life is being regenerated, as is the purpose of the penetration of the penis. I am every woman. I am every human. The wounds and sufferings of life can be replanted and the unpopular can be valuable. It is through the consciousness of this darkness that I know compassion; it is through this consciousness that I can understand myself and other people from the inside out.

The young sister tells me she must be still to receive the giant penis. "Be still and thou shall know the eye of God," says the Old Testament. It is in the stillness that inspiration, creativity, and the deepest knowing can come to be. As T. S. Eliot expressed it: "At the still point of the turning world. Neither flesh nor fleshness;

neither from nor towards; at the still point, there the dance is . . ."
On the personal level it is experienced as a defense against pain—
be still and it will not hurt. On the archetypal level, in the spiritual
realms it is the quiet fertile ground of wisdom required for the
creative principle, the soil of transcendence. Create, regenerate,
inspire, and at the still point of being experience the deep Self. Feel
the rhythm of the universe and know, in timelessness, all is well.

Suffering, the great equalizer has always been a potent wake up
call. Transgressions, trauma, and abuse can be motivators for that
most important search—the one into our very nature. They can
also be doorways into the marrow of our beings and deliver us to
that which we most ardently search.

PART THREE
Undoing

REALIZATION

AND MYSTERIOUSLY, WITH ALL the digging and reflection up to now, the real work of waking up to the divine's knowing of itself through the human experience could begin. I had lived a full human life of sorrow and accomplishment—a life peppered with some real connections and unending neediness—an ordinary life seasoned with a family and a ceaseless yearning for what is real, what is true. And now, as if some wisdom revealed itself, it was time to let go. Let go of the accumulated beliefs, clung-to memories, assumptions about myself and life, and identities I had clothed myself in, used to "fill out" my human form. With all the accumulated wisdom and contributions I was still suffering. I was very connected to my human form, perhaps even more so having rounded out my personality in a gratifying way. Without being able to fully form how it now looked to me I was mystified that I didn't feel better inside; that I, with all the work and growth I had managed, still ached and felt adrift and shaky. It is in retrospect that I can see the readiness that revealed itself in me as enough veils had lifted and I became ripe.

DECEMBER 2007

I pick up *The Sun* magazine during a break between patients, (I am a clinical psychologist by profession) and come to an interview at the front of the magazine and read it thoroughly. I wonder about this man, Adyashanti, and am captivated by something I cannot name. I say to myself, *I have found a teacher*, when, in fact, I was not aware I was looking for a teacher, or needing one.

He speaks about enlightenment and awakening from the deep sleep of being human, and believing ourselves to be separate and alone. Wow, here are words that speak to that place inside me that has been looking and looking, and calling it all sorts of different things.

I find out he is very well known, widely followed, and he holds satsangs (meetings of people looking for what is most deeply true and abiding) and retreats where I live.

I begin to go to Adya's satsangs often and have the same type of experience each time. Even sitting in silence with a crowd of people, sitting still with my eyes closed, before Adya sits in his seat at the front of the large room, everything in me begins to open wider and wider. This pleasant physical sensation intensifies when Adya comes into the room and pretty much stays with me for the duration of our time together. If the room wasn't crowded I would lie down on the floor resembling DaVinci's *Vitruvian Man*. Arms and legs spread wide akimbo. Back flat on the floor, still and quiet. I had never felt this before—really, literally—I had never felt safely open and unguarded in the physical world, not even when alone, much less in the company of others, and strangers to boot! I enjoyed myself each time I went—rarely remembering what he had to say, even though during the time together I registered deeply recognizing the truth of what he was saying, and first and foremost, being touched by his presence.

I reach a crossroad, feeling a definite pull towards full awakening. I give serious consideration to finding a spiritual teacher. Somewhere along the way I discover that Adya no longer works with individuals and when the time comes to act I surprise myself by choosing to go into back into psychoanalysis.

BEING REBORN IN THE CRYING ROOM

BEAUTY HONES

"So many tears behind these words.
Love hones like that—
perfects and
purifies
the
gift."

ST. THOMAS AQUINAS
Love Poems from God

I dream:

I see my back. I am in front of my home and I am dressed as if I am living in India, with a sari. There is a clothesline hanging across the courtyard anchored by both sides of the L shape of the house. All the clothes on the line are also saris and other articles of clothing worn in India. I am looking at the house knowing I am about to lose the entire home. I am bereft and as the feeling of loss sits in me I feel myself torn open from my pelvic area to the top of my head. The feeling is almost too intense to bear, and it wakes me up.

There is a home theme to many of my dreams. They seem to follow the theme of discovering and destroying the home of the false self. Throughout my life I had a re-occurring dream where I discovered a wonderful new house or the one I lived in, much to my delight, had many, many undetected rooms, nooks, and crannies. I explored to my heart's content. They speak to a desired discovery, one of knowing myself. They speak of the profound desire of discovering true home.

And then, I had two big dreams where my home is destroyed, first when I left my marriage and now, in analysis, with a conscious intention of letting go. And both times the loss is overpowering and immensely emotional. Surrender of, letting go of the conditioned self is visceral. Something inside, likely my ego, is registering the serious devotion and willingness to surrender.

40

Throughout my life I have also, in an even deeper and more real way, seen "home" as a symbol of oneness. I looked for home; I wanted to go home; I longed to return home. Be home. My heart soared at the word—home! The recognition of home is visceral and profoundly restful.

I am in analysis three times a week for four years, and I cry in every single session. I literally cry each and every time with grief and pain, and I wonder if it will ever stop.

But I feel myself slowly letting go, little by little, moment by moment. There is a sensation inside that resembles opening a clenched and tight fist. The more familiar I become with my emotions, the more words I have to describe being angry or sad, or feeling sorrow and rage. The more intimate I become with myself, the more confidence I develop in seeing whatever needs to be seen. In the company of my wise and skilled analyst, the more defenses and layers I genuinely lay at our feet. Not denying or avoiding any feelings—raw and unceasing—and being in the deep questions—afraid of what? What does being angry say about who I think I am? What beliefs run my life? What exactly am I protecting? It is both terrifying and liberating to face squarely and honestly how I feel and what I believe. I have a sense of an authenticity I have long yearned for. I am honest with myself and I am honest with my analyst. And it feels like brand new territory.

Sitting with my analyst in a safe environment I frequently get very, very quiet—I am still and open, naturally. And then I contract, fear grips my gut, and I protest mightily. I scream "no" in a thousand different ways. I will not and cannot let go.

Behind and underneath our beliefs, our identities, our roles, and our memories lie the rawness and the purity of our constrictions—our human emotional response to what we have experienced, and are experiencing in our lives. From the time we are infants and children we cover over the immediate sensation of pain. But the pain does not go away.

In the safe arms of a skilled and warm therapist I am able to get direct contact with these deeply buried, repressed, and dissociated feelings. This is the beginning of a conscious dedication to letting go. I am allowing the beginning of the dismantling of the façade, the inauthentic face I have overused.

"There are some people who have had extraordinarily difficult times in their lives—who have experienced traumatic events that may have caused an even deeper grasping at this root level of being. For these people, the grasping at the level of the gut may be reinforced as they come closer to a deeper stage of consciousness. If this is the case for you, it is important not to force anything. You may need specialized help to deal with this aspect of awakening; it may be necessary to find some way to address the deeper sense of trauma you are experiencing before you will be able to let it go. If this is the case, I recommend finding somebody who truly knows how to deal with such experiences, how to meet them in a useful way. You will know that the approach this person is offering is useful because it will start working. This root level of grasping will start to let go."

ADYASHANTI
The End of Your World

Even though I had been following Adya for a couple of years I did not see this excerpt until long after finishing analysis. And I see, in retrospect, how I intuited what I needed, as well as gained an enormous respect for a kind and slow uncovering of the many layers of protection I had put into place to not feel the most tender places inside me—the places we all spend lifetimes avoiding feeling and knowing about, and which we certainly keep hidden from others. With great regard and respect, I am beginning to have a sense of the impact of trauma on my body and psyche, and how trust, real trust, is needed for the body to unwind. I am beginning to have more respect for how things can slowly and gently unwind when the underlying call for waking up is revered and followed.

Let me say something here about being vulnerable. For the most part we humans will do anything to avoid feeling vulnerable or to have our hearts break. Our culture mirrors our dislike and fear. Our misguided culture insists that healing, growing, and

42

living are supposed to feel good. And that strength has nothing to do with tenderness or rawness.

I found the opposite to be true. In fact, the closer I got to the truth of the matter, to facing the absurd flimsiness of my many masks and costumes, and to seeing and feeling the messy darkness of buried emotions within as they came to the light of day, the more the healing process intensified, bringing even more discomfort. Indeed, my days, weeks, and months in analysis were very uncomfortable. As I came closer to being more awake, I became more sensitive. I was increasingly less numb, and I was less willing to turn away. The more intimate I became with my emotions, with all that I had removed myself from, and with those things I had labeled wrong, negative, bad, and chaotic, the more uncomfortable I became. But I have come to appreciate this sense of vulnerability as something sacred, as an intrepid truth teller.

THE BIG STUFF

A year into analysis I am diagnosed with breast cancer—for the second time. I am recovering from a double mastectomy when a friend brings me Jan Frazier's book, *When Fear Falls Away: The Story of a Sudden Awakening.* Jan's awakening came in the wake of several breast cancer scares and her presence and writing spoke very deeply to me. I was opening as I read her every word, opening in the same way I do when I am sitting with Adya. I felt my heart, my shoulders, and my gut loosen and relax as I read.

Before the cancer surgery I had a dream:

I see a parade of magnificent black horses, two abreast, (don't you just love the divine's sense of humor) at least fifteen to twenty horses, march regally along a pathway in England's countryside. The horse's manes and tails are adorned with ribbons and flowers—this is no usual, every day parade. I am keenly aware that the horses are walking past me—they are moving by and not stopping. This is important to realize. They are walking by and when they are out of sight I get into an orange Volkswagen bug and drive off.

I sense I am not going to die from this cancer or at this time.

But the pain of surgery is monumental—and so much worse because I am terrified. I give into the fear and the pain, and allow my friends and family to help me and be there every step of the way. I am in a living hell—all the more so because I know that it is fear that is dictating everything. And fear takes over completely. I am not aware of any thoughts (there must be some lurking) only the sensation of my body ravaged by a knife. I shudder.

I get infections and then reactions to the antibiotics—I cannot work for five months.

Something inside me gently holds my feet to the fire and says *do not look away*, so I don't. Squeamishly I change the drains coming out of my breasts and the bandages from my stomach. I cannot move from the couch because of pain and fatigue, and I stay honest with myself about how miserable I feel. There is nothing pretty about this experience and very little feels right. I am angry at the plastic surgeon for telling me that I would be back on my feet in no time at all and I feel overwhelmed with pain and fear. But I do not fall back into pretense and stay true to how it really is for me day by day.

One of the things that struck me throughout this difficult healing process was that, in spite of how awful I felt, I also felt alive and present. I suspect it had to do with the work I was doing in analysis, which gave me access to language for how I felt. I was less beholden to my defenses, maybe even less defensive. This did matter, I did hurt, and I didn't have to hide. I was able, to some degree as it was happening, to unclench my gut and open my fists.

As the days, weeks, and months passed, I became aware of a feeling of tenderness deep inside me. It tastes sweet, welcome, and comes about quite naturally, and my body, at last, begins to finally knit back together and heal. The pain and rawness recede. When I am finally back at work my stamina increases. I acclimate to a new body. I begin to inhabit my body, aware that I am not as dissociated from my shape and bodily sensations as I had always been.

UNCHARTED TERRITORY
NOV. 20, 2011

My analyst misses three of our regular appointments, for one reason or another, and she doesn't show up. The first time this happens I am sitting in the waiting room and I watch as the time comes and goes when she should come and get me. I knock on her door and I try the knob, but the door to her office is locked. I go home, as if in a dream. It doesn't feel real or perhaps more to the point I don't feel anything and so being forgotten isn't really registering.

When we get together the next time she tells me how sorry she is; she had a family emergency and completely lost track of time. I have the sense, in some ways, she feels even worse than I do. I am aware of being upset on the fringes of my consciousness, but the upset doesn't appear to linger.

The second time I had just gotten home after being out of the country for five weeks. I had seen her on Skype while I was gone so our regular routine wouldn't be disrupted. When I get home we have a couple of in-person sessions the first week. I arrive for the third session of that first week, but she doesn't appear in the waiting room and her door is locked again. I wait outside in my car, wondering what to do when I see her pull up and park down the block from where I am sitting, so I get out and approach her on the street. I suggest to her that there has been a mix-up and it seems she has missed our appointment. It's so funny to me that what I was most aware of is how present she seems under the circumstances. She doesn't appear distressed. We talk it over and decide to meet for the remaining time left.

I sit down in her office aware of being upset and rattled, but I am too scared to say so. I can see the flurry of emotions inside my body and mind. At the same time I also believe I understand—while I was away we met twice a week, and this is our third meeting of the week (now that I am home). It was an honest mistake, but I don't remember what we talked about for the half hour session we had that day. By the next day I appear to be no longer be upset.

The third time, I am sitting in the waiting room and I can actually feel the vacuum ahead of time. When she doesn't show up

I just know she isn't coming and I am incredulous. *Really, how is this happening? A third time—honestly, that is simply not possible,* I say to myself. I am immediately and unequivocally angry, furious. I wish she would show up just so I could scream at her right there and then.

I go home, wait for her call, and miss it when it comes. I inadvertently erase her message. I am angry at her, naturally and spontaneously loosening something in me that brings an odd sense of relief. But the biggest storm is the existential vacuum and despair I sink into—with no safety net or buffer from the horror and terror of no boundaries, no floor, no ties, or tether. It is the experience, the felt sensation of feeling abandoned. I feel unspeakable, incomprehensible terror in every cell of my body, and there are no words to soften it.

There is something familiar about the feeling—something about believing I am truly alone, hanging on for dear life, as a child who cannot survive on her own. And knowing I experienced this as a child but could not feel it, not for one minute, it is incomprehensible to me how anyone or I can live through this.

And oddly, so oddly, I am gladdened to be here, in this raw and primal place. Like an undigested piece of rancid food that needs to take its natural course, there is a deep knowing that it took getting close to my analyst in a visceral and real way, coming to depend on her caring for me and then feeling the unspeakable loss of apparently losing her or having her forget me.

I tell her "this is what I came for"—feeling this deeply.

I am present for it all—the intense and full-bodied state of emotions, the sense of unbearable loss and terror, as well as feeling something else operating here, something familiar, like an alright-ness, maybe even like a helping hand.

PEEKS IN—DOORS OPENING

I am sitting on my bed, staring at the walls and filled with these terrifying emotions of abandonment, heavy, scary, and overflowing. Something inside me moves, and following an intuitive instinct I go outside and sit under the blanket of stars. I shiver in the cool air and lie down so I can spread out under the sky. The pain and suffering begin to dissipate, actually begin to evaporate. I am so surprised, delighted to watch as peace begins to fill the spaces around the emotions and even fill the crevices of my mind and body. I have not experienced anything like this before; not being held hostage by pain and suffering feels magical. I think so much so because the process of evaporating happens naturally.

A few days later I again notice strong feelings of anger and rage. My limbs and jaw are tight, tense, and painful. I have nightmares; I have an image of a dragon spewing fire over a vast land.

There is an intense anxiety in my chest, sitting there for a full day. There is a build up in the top of my head, like it is going to ex-plode. I realize it is rage and I feel full to the brim with the pressure of it. My legs are tense and I want to stomp my feet, like a two year old having a tantrum. It is scary and intense. The lid is open and touching these feelings I feel tremendous anxiety—I have night-mare after nightmare.

I listen to the music of Handel's "Messiah" and feel despair—a deep sense of there being no one there. I am in the full experience with no buffer. I am open, oh so open, to feel the full impact of being alone in the fullness of yearning—I watch it engulf me and move on. I feel like I am going to die from want.

I am beginning to touch and feel anger. It is scary and at times overwhelming to me. I am aware of both the physical sensation of strong emotions and also of being afraid to feel them—a some-times subtle and sometimes strong resistance to the feelings and to the sense I carried of myself—crushing the pride I had in be-ing gentle.

Presence is becoming more palpable. By being guided to the sky and stars, presence is becoming more active and accessible in an everyday way. I feel like I am going to die from want. If we are fortunate we will die from want. We will recognize the longing for what it really is—a call to surrender the small self and die into our true being.

* * *

There is a strong build up of energy inside—I feel it in my limbs, especially my thighs. I originally thought it was restlessness, and now watching and feeling the intensity come and go, right below the most conscious awareness (I cannot touch it or feel it), but know it is there—a feeling of calm and well-being that makes me giddy to even think about or anticipate. Something is coming more to life inside, little by little.

There is freedom in being it all—and knowing I feel sad, angry, happy, impatient, and so on as awareness of the divine's presence grows inside me, and it's okay. I am not immune to my emotions and reactions and it is okay. I am not as afraid of feeling anymore. I am not afraid to feel fear—no small potatoes.

* * *

When I first went into analysis I boldly stated: "My spiritual life is off the table." Who knew what I really meant by that, what exactly I was protecting, and why it needed protecting? What I do know is that slowly, but surely, I entered a long, dark night of the soul—one without God and without belief. It meant feeling without a mental concept of "this is for the highest good," or "something is watching over me," as a protection. It meant including the possibility that my connection to something more, to the invisible world was an illusion. Oddly it was both horrifying and liberating.

Questioning, genuinely questioning my belief in God was a big deal for me. This belief appeared to be my sole lifeline, my when-all-else-fails place to go, especially since my heart had closed me off to most of this world. And yet, sitting in analysis, looking at my internal state, with the underlying commitment to seeing what was true and what was false, I had no choice but to see the belief as it truly was—flimsy and unable to hold much water when it really came down to it. It was magical thinking—somehow-things-would-work-out kind of thinking. The reality of presence and the invisible world had not been tested in this real way, not been allowed the room to mature.

I soon discovered that much of my belief came from a child-like fantasy that in the end everything would be well, meaning no pain, no harm, and trusting in a made-up view of how life should work; at least my life. I gave meaning out of a friend giving me earrings when the earrings were something I had wanted for a long time. Stretching the exchange beyond the pleasure of the gift to it meaning I was special and that life would treat me accordingly, sparing me pain and suffering.

This was a tiring night for my weary soul—having my hopes dashed over and over again as my analyst and I dismantled this magical thinking and untangled the places in my mind that were protecting me from direct feeling and living. Underlying most of these illusions was the desire to be taken care of—taken care of as a child is by a parent, when the child doesn't have to worry or be on its own. This child was very much alive in my being.

When it comes time to letting go of illusions, the ego (and the child) has a very strong opinion in the matter, finds every which way to say no, and tries to sabotage each and every attempt at questioning its authority. What held me in great stead throughout was fierceness for discovering what was real, what is true. In the darkest moments I would sincerely and sometimes out loud say to myself, "I know this is hard, and more than anything I am open, radically open to the truth."

NEW YEAR'S EVE, 2011

Somewhere I read or hear the phrase "drop the observer" and it resonates. Whether it means a psychological vigilance or a spiritual observer, it speaks to allowing oneself to experience and enter reality directly. As I am entering different feeling states with no filters, I can intuit moving through the world in direct contact—being connected to what is. It is a big step to drop into what I have always sensed but have not been able to touch, express, or really know.

There is a quickening of energy inside me. It is surging throughout my entire body with great intensity. I am moved to tears and laughter. I drive to my friend's home for dinner, and all by myself in the car I find myself laughing—for no apparent reason whatsoever, but oh my goodness, does it feel wonderful and free. I am on the phone with another friend and I begin to feel the upsurge of energy and begin to cry—and feel excited, relieved, and awed. Beneath, around, and under the walls and armor is enormous energy.

Life, pulsating energizing life is coming alive to itself. Under, around, and in between all the defenses, all the constrictions, the fears, the depression, and resistances is the energy of the universe—life expressing itself. It feels so good to laugh, to cry, and to move with the beginning of abandon.

I am having lymph massages as I had developed lymphedema after a couple of sessions of radiation from the first time I had breast cancer, and I notice the absence of pain. It is hard to notice absence—it is so much easier to be aware of pain. But I am noticing when I don't feel pain and I am aware, at times, of not being distracted by pain. There is more room to notice and know the absence of pain and suffering—the space around.

I look back now and can see how glimpses showed up—in this case it was a fleeting whisper of spaciousness. Somehow it got my attention, in spite of how easy it is to lose ourselves inside our busy minds and compelling conditioning. I had a momentary glimpse or taste of a larger reality.

A Presence is Making Itself Known
January 1st, 2012

I dream that I am nine months pregnant, in a full wedding gown and veil, waiting and preparing for marriage.

I dream that June, my beloved first analyst and mentor, shows me her two paintings. In the first one she is facing forward and is surrounded by color. The next painting stuns me with its power. She is facing away, with her back to me, sporting large magnificent angel wings and surrounded by deep vibrant colors in an abstract palette. This brings to my mind L.'s painting (a woman I know) and I realize the difference in the palette of colors is that June's is integrated.

I notice being more and more present, a stark contrast from being dissociated and cut off from myself. I have less of an undertow pulling me into dark inner places and I feel more awake and alive. More integrated.

I marvel at being alive, especially since I have been depressed most of my life and have been exhausted from the pretense of keeping my chin up. I marvel at being real and honest about how I feel.

I suspect many people who have known me throughout my life might be surprised to know I was chronically depressed. For the most part I had a façade of friendliness, could hide my moods from the outside world, and I had an impressive ability to accommodate whatever the social requirements were. However, I was never mistaken or fooled about my inner state—the dark undertow.

CHANGING GOLD INTO CURRENCY

My outer world continues to reflect a coming-and-going inner state of disharmony—no sooner am I healed and recovered from breast cancer surgery than I find I am in a financial crisis. A friend has been my financial advisor—watching over and investing my retirement portfolio—an inheritance from my mother. One weekend morning, over breakfast, she tells me her profound worry and concerns about the possibility of a catastrophe in our world. To her, the end of the world is lurking in a real and immediate way. It is not the first time she has voiced this kind of thinking, but it is the first time I truly hear the terror in her voice and her conviction that she and her family are not safe. I listen as she relays her survival plans, including taking her beloved cat's life before taking her own. I hear, for the first time, the profound helplessness she feels.

I am shook to my core for many reasons. Is she really going to take her life? Should I do something or try to reason with her? What effect are her fears having on her life, her choices, on her ability to make clear decisions? How has her fear and paranoia affected her care of my money? How safe is my retirement fund and what will happen to our friendship?

I begin to take on every nook and cranny of my financial life, paying attention to how investments work and what my particular portfolio does and doesn't do. I seek out people in the profession and get their advice about my situation.

I vacillate between terror and empowerment. I feel intense rage—shocking and ugly. Money stays a big issue and I keep all the moving pieces in my sight.

I had given over my portfolio to my friend so I could be taken care of. I did not want to think about money—so I let her do whatever she thought was right. Several years ago an outside advisor looked at my portfolio and said she had never heard of any of the products my friend had invested my money into. A mutual friend suggested if I said anything about this to the friend who was doing the investing, it would hurt her terribly and cost me her friendship.

I get on more solid footing through lots of legwork and by staying attentive to all the details of my finances. I make sure I really understand what people are telling me and ask question after question until I am clear.

I have an honest and frank conversation with my friend telling her I can no longer have her as a financial advisor. I am able to have this hard conversation without any emotional charge. I am well aware of the dance we have both been dancing so I can, without blaming either one of us, be very clear about needing to change the situation. She is upset but seems to understand enough and handles the meeting professionally.

I feel good as I learn how to handle my finances.

I find a local advisor for my annuity and she calls to alert me about a discrepancy in funds between what I thought I had and what I really did have. I am standing in the kitchen with the phone to my ear, I feel the breath leave my body, and know from the inside out what it means to fall to your knees. I had nothing holding me up, nothing between me and the stunning reality of how asleep I had been. How thoroughly and completely absent I had been in terms of paying attention and letting someone else rule my affairs. I had possibly lost a lot of money but more vital, in some underlying way, I had been sleepwalking all my life. And the chickens were coming to roost.

And, to compound matters, I am in the middle of a slump in my practice—two months now in the red, with little cushion. It is common for people to come and go in therapy, a practice vacillating between full and less full. Therapists learn to ride these waves and financially live accordingly. Now, for the first time in my career almost half of my patients are ending therapy at the same time! With the help of two supervisors I look for any extenuating issues that might be contributing here. Nothing, other than an odd perfect storm of reasons people needed to end treatment, including national economic crises, reveals itself.

I had used my savings while recovering from cancer surgery and now I am not sure how much I still have in my retirement fund. I am anxious and slightly in shock, but it is secondary to the strength of watching and paying attention.

I feel expansive in the midst, and when I feel a deep sense of freedom my mind goes to *now you can buy something or now it will be alright*, and in the same moment I remember that that is not true. I do not have enough money and my feeling of freedom and expansiveness is not because I will necessarily have enough money or because of some fantasy—it is the place of doing what I need to do for the situation I am in—staying true to reality and staying planted in the here and now.

I walk to Fillmore Street and begin to feel sad and deprived. It is hard to walk by all the stores knowing I cannot even think about getting anything. It is hard to live here with no puffs of clouds, false reassurances, or childlike fantasies.

What shows up though is a close and immediate connection with what is real—no buffers, and no distance between me and what is. That means I feel the raw emotions and face my problems without a belief in magic endings. I actually like being honest with myself; there is enormous relief in living from what is true.

The financial crisis resolved over the next year, in part because I stayed alert and conscious to what I had and what I didn't have. I noted every penny I spent, putting myself on a budget for the first time, and not spending what I didn't have. And then, over a period of a year or so, my therapy practice grew enough to provide me, once again, with a living to allow me to begin depositing into savings. I got an accurate understanding of my retirement portfolio, and even though I didn't have as much as I had thought I had, I learned that the policy I did have had good benefits and it was a good idea to stay with it. And an even better idea was to stay in touch with my new financial advisor.

I was grateful that I didn't lose all my finances—I don't think I fully registered what it might have meant to become destitute. In retrospect, I see once again, the letting go happening in stages. I didn't fully register what it might have meant to lose all my money. I lived within the reality of what was happening at the time—I didn't have to know what it would have been like, really like, to be without enough money.

JANUARY 29TH, 2012

I had a three-hour reverie/spontaneous processing in the middle of the night. I saw myself as an edifice of solid ice—filled with hatred and rage. I felt relief in seeing what is going on and felt the impact of the intense emotions.

I saw a river with ice floating and beginning to break up. I could feel myself thawing inside.

FEBRUARY 1ST, 2012

I am aware of an internal screaming, hungry baby who thinks she is going to die, the existential terror for my ego facing psychological death, the remembering, the knowing "I am going to die."

I awake in the middle of the night finding/imagining myself at the edge of the Grand Canyon and the terror takes my breath away. Compared to the Grand Canyon I am this very small being, sitting at the edge of this enormous cavern, my stomach in knots, as it would be sitting close to the rim of a great, great height.

FEBRUARY 2ND, 2012

I dream of a dog in deep distress, barking and barking, as if its life depends on it, and then a sharp shot, like a gun. Someone from a high window in a surrounding building has shot and killed a relative's beloved dog.

I scream like I have never screamed before. It sounds loud enough to reach the moon. I scream loud and long, and wake myself up. I am thawed enough to be able to protest. Loudly!

I weep and weep—

I feel like I am free falling...

FEBRUARY 5TH, 2012

This is what I imagine my experience was as a child, free falling from not being held sufficiently—having, at any given moment, no one sufficiently there to bring me into being, give me a sense of being, no caressing hands to bring me comfort and stability, and no sufficient consciousness to convey clarity, or help me to make sense of earth or life. I felt the utter terror of falling into what feels like non-existence.

And now, in a healing environment I have hands to catch me, eyes to watch and guide me, so I can let go, go where I have not gone before, and know I am not alone.

And deeper still, my ego, in the journey into awakening—faces psychological death, letting go, leaning into the Grand Canyon, the void—and this time there is a good, ample, gentle, and benign space living inside so I can let go.

FEBRUARY 7TH, 2012

Is there a design, destiny, or fate to our life? Parents teach children limits and behaviors to help them get along in the world and in their lives. They teach table manners and how to get along with their family and their friends. Children might not like the limits or the discipline; it might feel capricious, random, and meaningless. And yet as adults we will find manners useful in the boardroom, on the baseball field, and at home. As adults we find our ability to accept not getting everything we want useful in intimate relationships, and in living within our means.

Might this also be true on a cosmic plane? Are lessons there to ready us? Might my experiences of free falling, fear, and scary losses be preparations for a deeper letting go? Are there benefits to loss and to letting go that are not apparent when I am still a child spiritually?

There is a beginning awareness here. I am getting a glimpse into how insubstantial the small self really is. A house built on sand. When we sincerely look into and through beliefs, ideas, and defenses we see it is all nothing but a prop. It is all made up, like the program on a computer. It is fiction, like the people and circumstances in a novel—through and through.

This is such a liminal space.

The word "liminal" comes from the Latin word *limens*, which means, "threshold." It is when you have left the old way of looking, but have not yet been able to replace it with anything else. It is when you are between your old comfort zone and any possible new answer.

Seeing, feeling, and knowing the mind as a prop! What a revelation!

FEBRUARY 10TH, 2012

I have a phone conversation with a friend and tell her I feel untethered, unmoored—that the unmooring that has been going on in me for the duration of analysis is now showing up in the external world (finances). I tell her my experience of free falling and a sense of losing my identity/my mind. I tell her about the Grand Canyon and feel the sheer enormity and terror all through my body—I feel completely out of control.

Before falling asleep that night I have a knowing realization. I am not sitting at the edge of the canyon, looking over. I have fallen! I spontaneously see wings under my body cradling and supporting me in the fall. I fall asleep.

FEBRUARY 18TH, 2012

I have begun phone sessions with Jan Frazier, an awakened being of compassion and vastness, whose book, *When Fear Falls Away*, I had read while recovering from the mastectomy, and whose being moved me deeply. I had gone into analysis to wake up and become intimately friendly with my emotions. I tasted the delight of being present rather than frozen and guarded, and found the courage to live in and with what is true and real.

My talk with her this day is frustrating and disappointing in the moment. I had hoped to be transported and magically taken over by pure presence. Boy, oh boy, do our habits of the mind run deep, as does our longing for freedom.

She suggests that I am identified with what has been done to me and am living with "it should not have happened" when the freedom is in "it did happen." She is pointing to a deep surrendered acceptance. I feel a complete pull and a stranglehold of heels dug in as I internally fight and resist. Jan reminds me of the presence and vastness within me, and reminds me that my mother had the same in her. She tells me that my feelings will not kill me and that when I lie down on my bed it is deeper and deeper and will hold me all the way down.

I can let go slightly.

I awake at two in the morning from a dream:

A friend is at the bottom of a path and very much wants to come up to where I am standing. We are both aware of how vulnerable he is and being in such a fragile physical state he cannot approach the path without fearing he will hurt himself. I turn to another friend and ask if she can turn on the porch light so he can come up the path. I look back to my fragile friend and see he is carrying a fairly large lantern. He has the light to come up on his own but he won't.

I wake and know immediately that, in the dream, I am me and the friend. I sit with both of us in a semi-awake state and try to actively imagine helping him move and walk the path on his own. I realize I am revolted by his state and cannot stand him. I sink further into myself looking for a softer place and cannot find it no matter how hard I try. I am at an impasse and my body carries the full weight of both sides. I am tense, angry, and overly stimulated. There appears to be no resolution and no getting back to sleep.

I am moved with a knowing of what to do. I get up, put on a sweatshirt over my pajamas, grab my keys, and walk to the rooftop of my building, up three flights. I go to the nighttime sky, sit, and take in the vast spaciousness of the sky and stars. I feel reassuringly small. It is cold and beautiful. I lie down on the deck; it is wet and cold. I look up at the sky and take it in with no thoughts or ideas. I don't stay long and fall back to sleep immediately when I get back into bed. *I dream that a friend is calling me on the phone and she is in tears. "Have you read this week's assignment yet? Have you read the article called Amazing Grace?" I have not read it yet, but will, I tell her.*

I relay the dream to Jan—it helps to express it out loud.

FEBRUARY 20TH, 2012

I have cut back in analysis from three times a week to two. I wanted and chose this, and yet I feel furious with my analyst, as if it was her idea. I block her every attempt at reaching me. I tell her I know I am cutting off my nose to spite my face.

That night I sit with the emotions without fear—feel the rage, hatred, tension and pain. I feel a bone chilling cold—it is impossible to get warm. I am disgusted with how I am feeling and don't want to do this anymore.

FEBRUARY 21ST, 2012

I feel a sense of calm in letting the process and emotions flow through me, and feel an enormous comfort in having a bit more access to the vast spaciousness within that is in fact holding me. I am courting and surrendering into the vastness within as I work out the hard emotions with my analyst.

FEBRUARY 25TH, 2012

I look out my bedroom window and see and hear a young child of about four, crying hard and yelling at her mother. She is wearing a flourish of pink, stripes, and prints with her bike helmet. Her mother, seemingly hassled, is picking up dog poop with an inside out bag. She is holding onto a leash and the dog comes into view. In one sweeping motion she scoops up a boy of around one into her arms and with some free hand she lifts the child's scooter off the ground. The girl continues to scream and cry as the mother says something to her—seems to be of no avail since the child continues to loudly protest. The mother, with her hands full of the younger child, leash with the dog following, and scooter, begins to walk down the street—stopping every once in a while, to look back and call to the younger girl. The child has by now sat down on the street, legs outstretched, and continues to cry and protest, "I want it now." She says it with great seriousness—as if the mere shout of saying what she wants and when she wants it will make it happen.

I so get it! The cry of the wild, stricken child/ego—

And a different story—

My son and daughter-in-law's friends have lost their youngest child. He had heart surgery when he was one, had a heart attack, and died eight days later when he was two. He was the youngest of four and his next oldest sibling, who is four, is having a very hard time with his death. She crawled into his coffin, convinced his feet were cold, and that she needed to put socks on him. My daughter-in-law told me more recently that this four-year-old is having trouble going to sleep at night. She is afraid she will die. She asked her mother to please hold her so she can fall asleep, her mother said she would. The child asked her mother why she hadn't held her brother so he wouldn't die.

Even a mother cannot protect us from death. I feel a crisis of faith and I wonder—faith in what?

Everything in me, as a human, shuddered from even the idea of being unprotected, unprotected to the point of dying. Living inside the prison of my limited mind, I had the assumption that the experience of dying as an infant who is not adequately cared for and nourished would be terrifying. Within this liminal space it was impossible to embody the deeper reality of no death. It is impossible for our human mind to remotely fathom no death. We humans see ourselves as an entity, an entity made up of a body and a mind that is substantial and fixed—that will end and will die.

Our deepest nature, our true essence is awareness—awareness with no beginning and no end—formless and alive—vibrantly alive. The formless takes form—our bodies. The formless takes the form of consciousness—our minds and our bodies. We are the formless revealing itself—noticing itself—in its unbroken, unending vibrancy.

* * *

I continue to be up to my neck in shit in analysis—I am finding, feeling, and even revealing shame and humiliation—fury, rage, hatred, spite, and even possibly cruelty. I want to hurt my analyst. I am passively mean and cruel, knowing I am holding back from her. I am aware she is able to read and hold me and doesn't seem very bothered by my iciness, and yet I am humbled, taken aback, horrified by how mean I want to be, and how passively I look for ways that might upset her, hurt her.

I don't really succeed in hurting her. I don't really try all that hard, but I am in touch with something dark inside me. I sit with it and find perspective—I am able to not take it too seriously—I watch as I traverse raw and ugly motives and feelings—with and to someone I don't want to admit caring so much about.

FEBRUARY 26TH, 2012

I go into analysis and "have it out" once more with my analyst. I talk, in real time, about how I am feeling so tired of hammering her and being disgusted with myself. She invites me to recognize and feel the rage inside. I feel the ice-cold-to-the-marrow rage and the hate in the muscle pain and tension.

I feel surprisingly better when I leave. I am neither weighed down nor debilitated. The very act of seeing and feeling the rage and hate lightens the load. I am finding a foundation inside—I feel freer.

An advantage to being in therapy with a skilled and talented analyst is being able to show and express strong and challenging emotions without the analyst buckling under them or retaliating. For those of us who grew up with weak caregivers, who, because of their own pain and wounding were reactive and hurtful in the face of our loud screams, our pain, and our needs, this even keel acceptance of strong emotions and feelings is redemptive and transformative.

* * *

Before going to sleep I go to the sincere place of asking what is true—what is real. Please show me what is true, even if it is unpleasant or uncomfortable.

When I went to the grocery store today I became aware that I don't feel so mad at my analyst. At this moment I feel tired of holding on and ready to leave it behind.

That night I dream:

I am in the beginning of an intimate embrace and soon into it realize we need to have a conversation. He knows I had cancer and surgery but most likely doesn't realize its implications.

As I tell him, thinking I am talking about the physical implications I realize he is registering something I have not—we are talking about life and death. He pulls away and begins to tell me a story—about a woman he has been involved with—a Jennifer B-I-E spelling the name out to me carefully. I can tell from his bearing and tone that Jennifer died and he is very sad.

I wake up with my jaw clenched . . .

I let it loosen and feel deep sorrow. I see myself tightly curled and cry. Let it die, let it be!

As I look back I can see the many moments, like this dream, where my unconscious was picking up on the ego's impending death. The more recent dreams are benign and matter of fact while the earlier ones were more violent and terrified. Perhaps my ego is getting the message and is protesting.

MARCH 3RD, 2012

I am walking down Steiner Street towards Union when my left foot gives out from under me. I have a moment of realizing I am going to fall and instead of trying to contort myself and stop the fall I give into it. I hit the cement and my purse and bags go flying. I assess my body before getting up—realizing I am not that hurt, even the scrape from hitting the sidewalk is minimal. I look around and am surprised there is no one around. I realize I am okay and walk on to my office.

That night when I get into bed I realize I had completely forgotten that I had fallen—it had not registered past the event itself and now I am aware that my body is very sore and pained. I cannot get to sleep. I am feeling frazzled—very likely more from forgetting that I had fallen than the fall itself.

The black hole of forgetting: the experience of falling and seeming annihilation—the state of forgetting, living asleep!

No one was there to see or witness it, so did it happen? Without someone seeing do we come into true being?

Forgetting: when we humans are traumatized we dissociate from our bodies and from the actual experience. The defense of dissociation is a brilliant mode of protecting ourselves from the unbearable pain and violations. What it also means though is the event or circumstance or felt sense is gone, like it didn't even happen. This is a response to how unbearable the event is, to a distancing from the fact that it did happen, and from the overwhelm of not being able to contain that it did. Instead the event freezes in place. It doesn't live, it doesn't grow, and it doesn't have any opportunity for becoming richer or healed. It is as if what happened and how you felt was put into a storage container in another part of town, another country, or even another planet.

It is forgotten and kept in the dark.

To be conscious of our wholeness though, we need to remember. Re-member, re-stitch what has been discarded and forgotten. All, every part of us needs to be known, seen, and brought to consciousness. We need to unpack the storage container, bring it all home so to speak, to reflect our full and undivided being.

What makes it possible to remember is compassion and a reminder of our true, deepest nature—oneness.

I tell my analyst that I am bone cold. She asks, "like being dead?"

I say "no, like existentially being without any connection, like floating in space, not registering—not touched, not held in place so I can feel and know that I do exist—I am real—events and people are touching me," describing to her what dissociation and disembodiment feel like to me. And then I remember. I did fall. No one saw me fall. I forgot and then I remembered and tell my analyst. I am coming into being, awareness is being known.

There is a supposed Jewish legend that tells of God touching us on our upper lip (forming the indentation) as we enter the birth canal, to make us forget. This speaks to the deeper forgetting, of leaving behind something important to remember. Hence the looking to remember is set in motion. In the deepest sense, what is forgotten? What beckons for remembrance? Unity, wholeness, our undivided self calls, whispers, bellows to us, if we listen.

When we listen, we hear—we know that something was left behind—we remember we are wholeness . . . we are undivided—what has been left out or forgotten is reclaimed, remembered, loved, and made potent by its recognition. We remember and reflect our pure beingness.

"God, Infinite Aliveness—cognizing me (and everyone and everything else) into existence instant by instant and this consciousness finds everything very good.

Selfhood as the continuing product of infinite lovingness, which to my never-ceasing astonishment takes the story of suffering out of even the most humanly 'unpleasant' situations, including the prospect of personal extinction."

JOHN WREN-LEWIS

Something is changing and I am not sure what. I am praying—and I am courting vastness, faith, and love—the real deal! I pray to be love—may I be love—intuiting something here that comes out of me naturally and easily—may I be love—not only glimpses, not limited to the experience with my woman's group so many years ago, not only here and there, but eternal love.

I am aware of lots of synchronicity—it seems to be happening more and more—"coincidences" that are getting my attention. I come out of the shower and choose to turn on the TV while I dry off, an unusual thing for me to do. I randomly channel surf, not paying that much attention and find a children's choir singing "Amazing Grace." It is beautiful and reminds me of the dream I had intending to read the assignment called "amazing grace." The children were at the end of the song when I tuned in, singing words I am less familiar with; ending with "grace will take you home."

May it be so!

FEBRUARY 21ST, 2012

I see a frozen planet program on TV, following a male polar bear looking for a mate, walking miles and miles over and through white snow—as far as the eye can see. He picks up a female scent and walks in that direction. He finds her tracks and the narrator tells us, "It is less tiring to walk in her footsteps."

This is my experience of transmission—how my body and soul opened in the presence of Adya and with Jan. Their being, their complete lack of defenses, and their unconditional love ignited the flickers and flames of presence within me. I could relax (less tiring) in their company, in their footsteps.

FEBRUARY 25TH, 2012

There is a lot going on internally these days. I am aware, in spite of knowing better, I want something irrational from my analyst. No matter how hard I try I cannot get her to love me the way I want her to, as I needed my mother to love me when I was a baby and a child—reminding me of the knock-your-head-against-the-wall attempt to change the past or live as if it is happening right now— here is a chance to accept who my analyst is and what she can and cannot give me—and to let go of being so angry for what she is not able to do for me.

I am sitting with agitation—feeling frightened of even the prospect of not having therapy. I sit with all the feelings, not having to move anything or make anything happen, simply let it all percolate. I am also aware of being very low on funds and how much money being in analysis is costing me. Something tells me I am ready to leave.

MARCH 1ST, 2012

With great nerves and trepidation I broach the subject with my analyst about leaving therapy. She asks me if I had thought about when and I said I had not, only that I needed to begin the conversation with her.

That night I had a dream:

I am the passenger in a car with my father driving. It is real time and current. He appears very normal and real. I am lost in thought, relaxed, and thinking about mailing R.'s birthday present. My father and I are going somewhere for two days and I am figuring out how and when to mail the package. I realize that my father is shaking himself, from head to toe. I ask what he is doing and he tells me that he was beginning to fall asleep at the wheel so he was shaking himself awake. I am flabbergasted that I had not, in a vigilant way, been watching him. I wake up.

Do I dare get on with my life and not pay vigilant attention to my past? What about shaking myself awake? It is two in the morning and I am struck by how real my father looked—just like I would imagine him to look if he was physically here right now. I am with my father and I am not vigilant. I am relaxed!

I begin to think about my associations to my father and am mostly struck that he was unable to fulfill his potential. Shaking himself awake.

The call to our ultimate potential—recognizing what we really are. Shaking myself awake.

That, too, is striking in its realness and its clarity—not neurotic, scared, or reactive.

I wake up the next morning and realize I am going to end therapy this week and have two more days. Considering my financial situation it only makes sense to stop now. Stop spending extra while I don't have extra, not spending more until I am out of debt.

The next couple of days I have two more dreams.

I walk into a room and see a baby that is deformed in a grotesque, unreal way. It appears to be cocooned in a plastic blue casing, with its face located inside. I go over to the baby, even though

I am repulsed and sit down next to it. In very little time I am surprised that I have genuine fondness and caring for this infant. I see its face and make eye contact with it and feel kindness and caring.

In the next dream—*I see a former friend across the street and she walks across another street to pick up cleaning equipment. She goes back to where she was and starts to clean the street. I am so surprised since it is unusual for her to do menial work. I like what I am seeing. Chop wood and carry water!*

It is my last day in analysis . . .

MARCH 31ST, 2012

I am absorbing and assimilating the last four years. I am reflecting on my emotional life since the beginning of life here. I am feeling content, without any complaint including how I feel. I feel disappointment, anxiety, fear, and great anticipation—I am crying a lot. It all passes through me. I feel quiet inside.

I hear a consistent, quiet move towards stepping out onto a larger stage.

APRIL 7TH, 2012

I dream about my analyst leaving and when I awake it feels like further confirmation of our time together being complete.

I am in a home with a man, who has been my lover, and he, too, is going to leave. There is a great commotion outside and there is a wild animal threatening to attack. Inside the home, there is a gigantic insect scurrying across the floor. I wonder how I am going to fare living by myself. The man is sitting on the floor and he has done something for which I am grateful so I go over to kiss his neck and cheek. He indicates he would like a kiss on the mouth, and when I lean in to kiss him he kisses me with great intensity and indicates he would like it returned. I do so, and much to my surprise, he says my name, very clearly, distinctly, and deeply. I feel touched, moved and very curious as to what it means.

When Adam names the animals he is calling them into existence—they have been recognized and named. As have I!

APRIL 21ST, 2012, 3:00 A.M.

I have an appointment with Jan next Monday. It makes sense to talk with her through this transition and I am especially hoping for our contact to touch those parts of me that are opening to the transcendent/the vast/the divine. My young, magical thinking beliefs have dissolved to a large degree, leaving me receptive to what is present, what is true. I am looking to be in a mature, real, and integrated faith in God; and its energy, presence, and love that stays alive in my daily life—that I can be with these young scared places inside—needy and alone—reach out to my loved ones and find the fullness inside to also hold others and life. Knowing that I have received what I needed from my analysis, I fall to the bottom of the hole and find helping hands to climb back out over and over—giving myself new awareness that I am not alone, that my feelings will guide me to some knowing, that this larger force moving through our lives is intelligent and omnipresent.

I feel able to hold it all, to know the agony of pride, the child-like wanting to be loved everywhere and by everyone, the love of God, and the largesse that is big enough to dissipate humiliation and self-protection. I know the innocence of my ego's demand to be understood and stroked and I know the softness and depth of the mattress that catches me and holds me no matter how relaxed and far back I lie. I know the defensive anger and wanting to strike out—foul! And I know the vastness of the sky's changing color and movement as it surrounds my tiny clump of cells in a soft embrace and reminds me of something much larger.

MAY 6TH, 2012

I have a dream the night before speaking with Jan.

I am outside and realize there is a very large flood. The flood is so intense that I see a car floating by which tells me the seriousness. I see a friend inside a house and say to her "I have died, haven't I?" She says "yes you have."

This is another precognition of an impending ego death, or perhaps the revealing of the slow and steady ego death, by death, by death. It is the death by death of whom I believed myself to be, the death by death of the conditioned small self.

Jan reminds me of it not being at all about what I am thinking, planning, or asking for. I have a felt sense of what she is saying, and I realize the moments of being in direct relationship with reality can be happening all the time. This realization scares me and fills me with a profound recognition at the very same time.

She tells me I do not have to do anything—I can get a real sense of that truth. Life will move on its own. I think of the sport curling and how being in analysis has cleared the way of a lot of debris and given me a strong sense of what I feel and what is going on in my body—both opening the way to have life flow through me. Without hearing my dream she tells me that awakening could unleash strong emotions, upheaval, and bliss in me. By the end of the session I am filled with an enormous amount of energy—difficult to contain, in fact I say at the end of an hour that I need to end the conversation—I am bursting at the seams . . . I go for a brisk walk, moving with the energy. Also, my heart feels like it is physically growing and taking up more space in my chest.

In my mind's eye I vividly see a large butterfly wing, very dewy as if just coming out of the chrysalis with beautiful soft hues of color, fluttering, fluttering, fluttering.

It is very difficult to sit still. I cannot contain the energy.

Your hand reached in
          And sat gently on
                    My mind
Your fingers spread
As my heart's strings
          Shuddered and
                    Stretched
Strange sensations
          Pushing its edges
                    Out

Energy—wild—thousands
    Of horses running through green fields
As your hand silenced my
    Mind
And some invisible
Force field filled my body
    Pushed against
        Limbs to bursting
My heart filling
    My chest
A pain? A sensation? A realization
    Alive
    Life
Moment by moment by moment
Something straining the
    Contours of my body
Pushing, pushing ever outward
Full—strong—steady
Bulging the seams/the outer reaches
As a dewy wing
    Large—very large
    Radiant with soft hues
Flutters
Flutters awake

MAY 10TH, 2012

I am sitting in a class of colleagues, speaking up, quite uncensored and spontaneously. I am not used to being unguarded in a group situation. It is scary and exciting to be in the moment without censoring and being vigilant. It looks to me like half-baked ideas, not many fully formed thoughts. I am aware of being embarrassed and feeling filled to the brim with tears, expecting it to back up on me and probably spill out and over when I get home. And then, much to my amazement, the feelings simply evaporate, and I am fully present in class again.

Much of the time these days I have no idea why I feel what I do—and yet it doesn't seem to matter. It is like watching the ocean tide coming in and going out with fish, pebbles, life, and debris washing up and going back out.

Like a steady upheaval from deep inside me, strong currents of feelings—leaving me feeling like a ship being tossed and turned, up and over and around, and then something holding steady. Something is watching the anxiety, something recognizes the familiarity of the sensation, watching—watching as the anxiety spills over and other times something is aware of a presence. Presence is being aware of itself.

I am walking around slightly ungrounded—feeling not in control. I remember reading David Hawkins, an awakened teacher, saying if you feel you are getting close to a spiritual transformation make sure someone close to you knows what is going on. I check in with a friend . . . and at the same time I hear this voice in my head asking whether this is truly real.

I am watching thoughts and allowing life to flow through me. There is a process going on here, something inside, aware and present, makes room for thoughts and feelings, without adhering to them, without taking them all that seriously, not always but more and more so. This process is widening and expanding my insides.

MAY 21ST, 2012

I have a bladder infection and I am in pain. I am irritated, angry, and snapping at my friends. Really, no subject is of any interest to me and I cannot identify what I am feeling, I cannot say anything to help matters. I am bitchy and contrarian—and saying it out loud without knowing what gives. In this regard I am less hidden and less driven by safety-at-all-costs. I am not making nice and not trying to keep things pleasant—so bloody uncomfortable!

A lot of energy is going into the way I think I should be and even more energy is going into beating myself up for how I am. It seems puzzling to me to have this negativity be so alive and strong.

MAY 28TH, 2012

I experience life emotionally in my mind, body, and as an identity as a person—isn't that an understatement! I have moments, like walking down the street and feeling an upwelling of love, for no apparent reason. It comes and goes. Then last night, feeling very tired—I am aware of anxiety, my old friend. I get into bed worried that the tension and anxiety will mean interrupted sleep again. I sink down into the core of my being and begin to deeply cry—the kind that rocks the belly—with few thoughts attached I cry it out.

I wake up rested yet somehow still tired. I get up and have lots of energy. It baffles me. I feel a sense of excitement and happiness.

I go to the theatre in the Tenderloin district of San Francisco—a sketchy neighborhood I am afraid of. I get out of the car and walk into a huge, cold wind. Without realizing it I get more scared and shut down, my body contracts instinctively.

I spend the evening not being able to connect with myself or my friends, shut down. It is painful and confusing. We walk the streets of the Tenderloin and I am in a daze.

The play itself is extraordinary. The actors are all playing different roles of real people who live in the neighborhood. They had interviewed them, giving voice to their words, gestures, and personalities. Without a doubt it brought the neighborhood to life in its humanness.

I leave feeling moved and deeply, deeply sorrowed. I had felt each person so acutely. When we drive away I see ten or twelve sleeping bags, each one bulky with the outline of a person, lined up against the wall of Glide Church. I take them in differently—the play succeeded in giving them personhood.

It was difficult to be in this state, especially late at night and insufficiently rested.

I wake up with the sorrow gone. That was yesterday.

JUNE 9TH, 2012

I want to dive right in—bring to awareness the connection I feel to transcendence. I want to bring to life what is known but not given expression or visibility yet.

Last night I went to bed early, very sleepy. I have been sleepy a lot recently. And yet, I couldn't fall asleep. I tune into the inner world. I find a lot of energy coursing through—involuntary shakes, mostly in my legs but in my arms as well. I feel a pool of energy in my groin. I tune into the energy—it feels like life flowing and shaking awake—like something having been dormant and not active. I am reminded of Kundalini energy. I tune in further and my legs begin to shake. I tune in and feel currents of energy, over and over.

Yesterday, before this experience, I went to an exhibit at a museum. I fell into the beauty of the fashion and was attuned completely to each article of clothing. I "knew" before reading the signs that accompanied each piece what was being shown. I felt the emotional tone of most outfits and could feel the energy of what it felt like to create and wear it. I was in the outfit and in the tone. The beginning of what it feels like to be one with.

At lunch right after, my friend was preoccupied—I realized we were not deeply connected. I realized it but did not get caught up in it. Without any effort I experienced the disconnection and "hung out." When she dropped me off and I went inside I felt the pangs of loneliness and sadness. I realized instantaneously that it was from not having been sufficiently connected and the feelings dissipated and did not return. I went about my business and felt whatever else was going on.

I read an interview about an artist who paints the ocean. I could feel his words off the page and could feel the depth of his diving into the essence of life.

There appears to be something inside awakening, awakening to something universal and conscious through the heart. It is being experienced through feeling—I notice an evolution of awareness, an intimacy with the transcendent. There is more and more immediacy with each moment. Feeling/instinct/sensing is guiding me through. Staying with the unformed unknown—living into the feeling and body senses.

* * *

I cannot find the bottom of what I am so angry about. I have little to no patience for pretense—in myself or in people around me. I am filled with annoyance and frustration—wanting to yell "what difference does it make?" "Isn't it completely obvious?" Or "why are we talking about this?" I write this out and become aware of attention (in the name of simple noticing or idle curiosity) masking judgment, envy, jealousy, or some such hidden emotion.

And then it comes to light; the pretense in myself. I am now aware of my unconscious pretense of pointing at one thing and meaning another. Pretense!

I am able to see what is going on inside myself by paying close attention to my projections.

Writing all this out actually contains the energy. It takes pages and pages of writing this out to come to this place of what is true and the relieving feeling of whew!

JUNE 10TH, 2012

I wake up this morning feeling like a dam had burst inside—I am full of energy, almost uncontainable. How much energy is sucked away with the troubles of the mind and worries? I get up, squeeze an organic orange for juice, and go to the farmer's market on a beautiful day.

Something significant is happening. The energy that began pulsating in me a few nights ago was in my limbs. Now it is throughout my body—groin, heart, and head. I am reluctant to write—so much is alive, needs to be—not put into words.

I speak with Jan and feel a profound sense of energy flowing—my body feeling porous and dissolving into thin air. There is no sense of I even as "I" talked and listened. I want to make note of this as it is happening and at the same time I am disinclined to put anything into words or even description.

I spend the day trying to do "normal" things—I do not feel grounded at all. I still don't. What has held me is not there. There is neither a sense of identity nor sense of self. None of this is showing up as a problem. It is quite noticeable though.

JUNE 12TH, 2012

Proclaim
Exclaim
Cannot explain

Rubbing the sleep out of my eyes
A third eye showing
A glimpse
      A peek

Like the corner of a photograph lifted up
      The sensing of behind
Right there!
Right there!

Pure sensation
      No ending
      No beginning
A floating sense of no me

Energy coursing through
Energy free to flow

Like a river widening and overflowing
Beyond, beyond, beyond

I am nowhere
I am everywhere

A glimpse
Letting go, letting be
Inviting residence

JUNE 17TH, 2012

It feels like energy is being used to reconstruct my interior. The digestive tract is tender, energy coursing through my system possibly rearranging mass. There is energy in my groin, pooled and pressured. There is no thought or desire alongside this—only pressure, like the energy needs to move.

If I give the benefit of the doubt to my body and felt sense responses I can see that unless there is a genuine need or direct emotional connection, I am not engaged in the same way—in fact, I have little to no interest in being engaged without a genuine need or direct emotional connection. This is so different from how it has always been. My own neediness, my own insecurities had dictated everything before. I stayed engaged whether I wanted to or not—so much effort, so much frustration, and so much dissatisfaction.

I just read in Jan's book about the oddness she felt when she registered indifference and I remember her saying something along those lines to me last week on the phone. Not to be surprised when I feel neutral—and that I might begin to have a different perspective on things.

JUNE 22ND, 2012

How to put into words this moment's experience . . . I am lying in bed, settling in for a night's sleep, and spontaneously my consciousness goes to "look" at my past. As if awareness behind me was looking to see what was there. There is nothing there—nothing at all, it is a pleasant, quiet void—an open space with no inkling, whatsoever, of "my personal history." I felt peaceful and oddly not at all surprised, either by the looking or by there being nothing there.

I can sense my ego hanging on, even while a deeper knowing in me remembers the ease, peace, and wellness of no self. The mind takes up a lot of space right now, with many complaints, judgments, distancing, irritation, and anger. The deepest sense I have is to let it all ride; even the voice that says this is sad, wrong, and too bad.

"Awareness is freeing itself, over and over and over"

ADYASHANTI

There is nothing holding me back these days. I have lots of freedom and space to explore, surrender, and let this process unfold. Other than work there is no structure at the moment. I am free to fall. Free to let go. Scary free. Open space. No one, nothing required.

JULY 17TH, 2012

I am back in a struggle. I have not written for a long time. I am reactive, oh so reactive, sitting with a silent scream—wishing I could explode and feeling held back, like I am squished in, pulled into a way-too-tiny place of fear and control. This brings me to an ice-cold fury. I go underground, internally, retreating into a place of "my own" where I cannot be reached—cannot be touched. And I am miserable because I am closed-down and off.

I want to be open. I now know the joy and freedom of openness. But in the presence of terror, perceived danger of being swallowed whole, or taken to a tiny fearful place, I recoil and shut down and off. It is a vicious cycle.

Here I am at four in the morning, not able to sleep. I have a headache and an upset stomach. I can feel slightly buried fits of rage and a lump in my throat. The reactions have become too oversized for watching. I am feeling overwhelmed, drowning in it, and not sleeping for being so upset.

So let's look now. What is real and true? Am I deluded? I want to scream and holler. I am sincere. I stomp my feet. Where did you go? And please, please can't you stay?

A house torn asunder cannot stand
A soul divided
A heart closed
All the while knowing.
Used to intuit

Now know
All the more excruciating to be closed off from . . .

JULY 19TH, 2012

on the cross
choice
choose

sliding into home
gentle slide into
an eternal address

open, open, open

the body bearing the brunt
of the made-up battle
tired, aches, head to toe—intestines
       letting go, letting go

open, open, open

a battle waged
what is scared?

Nothing to hold as fear evaporates

Slide, slide
The way is smooth, gentle

And above all
The eternal address
Real

    This was written after the latest session with Jan.
    Jan's response to my poem: "This is a made-up battle!"

* * *

I can feel the barriers dissolving, little by little. I feel a softening. Strong energy comes and goes. Feels like big, empty energy in my body—sometimes a rush of happiness, sometimes a feeling of needing to be in life, whatever that means. Sometimes it is not there. Sometimes—with some frequency—there is a strong pressure in my groin area. And sometimes a strong burning goes along with it. But mostly it is a pressure. It is like birth, an orgasm, and an outburst.

Everything seems intensified, heightened. When I am open and reachable, I feel it all—the picture of a sad man who has lost his son to senseless violence, my friend talking about the pain of a family member. Without anxiety or with lessened anxiety, everything is slower, quieter, and felt more intensely.

I feel lighter with fewer barriers.

July 27th, 2012

I am at ease when something breaks. I am at ease when I make a mistake and even to a significant degree when I am getting sick. I thought about it today: the catastrophe has already happened. The experience of being uncared for, not held, not sufficiently taken care of as an infant, the existential experience of falling through space, knowing neglect, and the horror of going through it has already happened. And now I am aware, have felt it in my bones, lived through it, and had it witnessed in a loving, caring, and attuned way—and so I am not subject to petty fears showing up as if they will lead to catastrophe. I have resources I did not have as a child. Some level of trauma feels softened.

August 7th, 2012

There is strong energy, like fire, inside me. I told a friend about this energetic fire and she recommended *Daughters of Fire* a diary by Irina Tweedie, taking us lucky readers intimately into her Kundalini awakening. I am feeling the fiery energy right off the pages. As if a transmission is taking place, it reflects the fire inside me.

While talking with another friend I am aware of my left arm feeling fiery, my chest is on fire, the top of my head and left side is pulsating with pressure.

My head is not clear. I feel in an altered state. I have felt that way off and on during the day today. Walking the streets knowing I am not very oriented or grounded. I remember this experience from a couple of months ago, speaking with Jan and telling her I feel ungrounded. That was before the significant experiences of being one with the exhibits in the museum.

It feels as if something alive is inside me, in my body. Moving. Right now there is a pressure at the top of my head.

I am finding a clearer "sight"—a simpler understanding of other people. I am at a restaurant and I want to say to the person waiting on me, "it is hard on you to have to be nice and speak sweetly even when you are not in the mood." It felt like a direct communication from her.

I am feeling outside of time—not grounded. I am continuing to read *Daughters of Fire* and I am feeling the experience from the inside out.

AUGUST 8TH, 2012

The truth is that I am still ego driven with glimpses and moments of something more transcendent. I am also aware of something loosening in my mind. I could say I am not as sharp as usual, but it feels more like I am not trying so hard or holding on as much. I feel a deep connection to surrendering—little by little and am aware of a background acknowledgment of annihilation.

The mind, which is fear, is reacting to surrendering—using the big barrel of annihilation, the big scary boogey-man.

AUGUST 9TH, 2012

I feel happy and present—an unleashing of a lot of energy inside. I am feeling alive.

Much of how I feel appears to be a consequence of analysis. I am attuned to myself, able to be present with what is real and immediate, and I have experienced falling in love in a deepening way . . . with my analysts, with Adya, with Jan. I realize in reading *Daughters of Fire*—her path is completely intertwined with the love and devotion she feels towards her guru. It doesn't really matter who the love object is, it matters that I can open to that power. This is the beginning of the opening of my heart.

Being with my grandchildren and adoring them. I do not take for granted being able to fully feel that and the spontaneity of it.

I had a night of dreams—I am angry in all of them. I feel slighted. I woke up to a couple of unexpected phone calls and requests, and feel ridiculously frazzled and angry. Like a two year old having a temper tantrum.

I want to bite off heads—who and what keep changing but the bite remains. The fact that the who and the what keep changing is what helps me more deeply recognize it is not anything external that is really getting under my skin. It is my internal assumptions and conditioned beliefs that I bring to the situations that trigger me. And it is the voice of "it shouldn't be this way" that prompts the constriction—and the constriction is what makes me feel miserable.

I "suffer" whenever I resist what is.

AUGUST 13TH, 2012

I do wonder if it is possible for me to live in an enlightened state permanently, meaning not being tossed about by these ego states. Jan said when I get sick and tired enough of the struggle I will give it up. She also said it is next to impossible to really know the other state when one is in the current. When I know the vastness and the silence there is no trace of my personal self. Now that I am living from the nuts and bolts and grievances of the personal self I can only glimpse and recall the sense and awareness of awareness.

I have no way of knowing whether it is real and true that working out the kinks of holding onto anger and getting through disappointments is important to my or any spiritual journey. Intuition has brought me through over and over and every time I look back

I see that it moves in the direction of growing and awareness. This has been a consistent and true unfolding of reality. I listen to Jan and she and other spiritual teachers all say we can become enlightened in a moment. My experience of a few months ago confirms that without a moment's notice or preparation I can fall into grace.

So, in the meantime since I am not living in that grace I can only remain true to what is in each and every moment.

As I write I realize I am not "hungry." I am not missing anything. I am very satisfied expressing what is.

And thank goodness for consciousness. My God, thank goodness for consciousness. That I can know this about myself, that I can be aware of the condition, the lack, and, to some mysterious degree, the unreality of it all.

I am lacking nothing. Right there is peace. Right there is the more and the all I have always intuited.

AUGUST 14TH, 2012

I am reflecting on being angry—the subject changes, but the feeling is the same. I can see that disappointment is under the anger—a deep lifetime pattern. Now I can begin to see that the instinct I have for "letting go" is here. Letting go of the grudges I hold onto. Letting go of the anger I feel when I am disappointed. Letting go of the expectation that is under the disappointment.

Truly living within the reality.

AUGUST 15TH, 2012

I feel fluid all day long. I am experiencing the joy and ease of being in the immediacy of each moment and with each person who comes into my office. Within me there is an ease of being real and being connected. I have the feeling that I am connected to something, something that flows like a current below the surface and guides all actions.

Interestingly, the surrender and letting go does not sugarcoat what I see; in fact, I appear to be seeing a bit more clearly, especially the essence of things and some people. Rather than turning me off or away, this clarity is helping me connect and relate in an immediate way, without having to protect, react, or distort.

AUGUST 18TH, 2012

I am reading *Daughter of Fire*—the part where she is breaking down and cannot bear it much more. She goes to her guru, who is holding his grandchild. The child looks at Irina and begins to howl. Irina is screaming at her guru who is holding the furious child, who is scratching at his face and arms. Irina cannot be heard over the scream of the child and falls to the ground sobbing. Her guru gets hold of the child and takes him into the house. Irina wonders how the mother did not hear and come running and thinks to herself, he always manages conditions as they need to be.

This reminds me of a similar state with my analyst—inconsolable—which reminds me of seeing a young child on the sidewalk outside my window, screaming, sobbing, and having a meltdown. And her observation of his being in conditions, as they need to be.

I remember thinking at the time this was no coincidence and now reading Irina's experience I too, can say the divine (direct reality) is behind conditions, as they are.

Noticing this, recognizing it, and knowing it—knowing myself, knowing the longings, the deep yearnings. This is the building of faith and trust, which is helping me into the total surrendering.

AUGUST 22ND, 2012

I have a quieter mind today—I see thoughts more as a vapor. I am noticing reactions without much connection. I can sink into a deeper place and feel or sense the calmness. I see the mind as a thin layer of soil, impure and crusty with overuse. I see deep layers of rich, vibrant, dark, and moist soil below.

I am still reading *Daughter of Fire*—"If a horse is going slow and another, a quicker one, overtakes it, the first horse, quite simply, gets wakened up. That is all there is to it . . . Why do we insist on satsang? Because it is a quickening. We do not teach—we quicken. I am stronger than you. So your currents adjust themselves to mine. This is a simple law of nature. The stronger magnetic current will affect, quicken the weaker."

This is my experience with Adya and Jan. Being in their presence quickens mine and awakens the presence within.

I feel a deepening of surrendering, an alignment into a deeper sense of being. A knowing—when the mind shows a judgment, an irritation, there is now a more automatic and, for the most part, an easier surrender, as if I am engaged in a marathon, well not quite a marathon, more a devotion to what is true that is already settled into and now being put into more practice.

In conversations I am aware of being directly engaged. The observer is quieting—perhaps the belief that I am separate is diminishing. I am listening to what is there—hearing what it is, as it is.

AUGUST 26TH, 2012

I went to Adya's satsang yesterday and it was very helpful. When I was sitting in meditation with him I felt the energy in me reach all the way to my throat. This is the first time it went that far. It began in my pelvic area, moved throughout my torso, including my arms, heart area, and up to the throat. I find I cannot really describe the sense of this energy. It is a pressure, light and gentle, but unlike whatever energy is typically in my body. I want to be able to describe it but I cannot.

I end up experiencing it. Then it leaves. Just like that. I was sad—felt sorrow. Later Adya mentioned, "trying to seduce grace"—I can so relate. "What can I do so grace will return?"

He spoke of being confronted with the totality of humanness along the way of the opening of spiritual awareness—the light and the dark. Using Buddha's time under the bodhi tree and Jesus' time in the desert as examples, both men came through without being tempted or resistant to all that they saw of themselves, all the demons. Yes! This is so helpful—all that comes up and how my worried thought goes to something that is wrong . . .

This gives me a deeper understanding and realization of what it means to be with what is, no matter what it is, and staying in the moment. Seeing the moment through and through, without resistance and, what speaks volumes to me right now and appears so important is seeing the moment without temptation or holding on.

I am seeing that the wanting to know how, as tempting and alluring as it is, boils down to resistance and wanting to have control.

* * *

I realize a misunderstanding I have of letting go. I believed it would result in a profound unity which, to be perfectly honest, meant, to me, never again feeling anything painful or difficult, an uninterrupted bliss. I realize now that each time I accept whatever I am feeling there is peace within and around that acceptance, and that is significant, that is unity.

I went for a hike with a friend—We came to a body of water near the ocean . . . along a trail and we stand together looking at the water. It, the water, is amazingly quiet. I hear the silence and feel the resonance inside—I can actually feel the silence inside. The silence is luxurious and moves me deeply.

I am continuing to read *Daughter of Fire*—her time, her experiences, and her personal work leading to deeper and deeper self-knowledge is so similar to my time in analysis. Know thyself. She plumbs her feelings, bravely facing each and every big and little humiliation, pain, discomfort, and especially her depth of loneliness. I am oddly comforted—yes, this journey is about feeling deeply and fully, without kidding yourself or running away . . .

SEPTEMBER 3RD, 2012

I dream,

I am getting married—there is a sense of beauty. There are crowds around me; they seem like people I know—all having other things to do or tend to. At some point I realize people were not gathering and the wedding will not be witnessed. I feel an enormous grief and turn to see my father there—I lean into him and begin to sob on his chest, while realizing I am surprised to find my father when I had expected my mother.

84

For years I have longed for a wedding dream to signify the wholeness of inner marriage. I have had a few through the years and each one is interrupted for one reason or another. In that regard this is another of the same. In this one, the pain of grief and longing harkens back to the dream I had when I entered into analysis—the breaking open from grief. The intensity of this dream was less than that one but strong enough to wake me up.

The longing—oh, the longing. The longing for the dissolution of self into the arms of the divine. The longing for my heart to be cracked open by love. The longing for oneness, the melting into life. The longing for stillness.

I have moments of calm and well-being and then, often without any preamble or apparent reason, I experience an unpredictable fall into the dark. I am sitting at Starbucks reading *Daughter of Fire*. Her teacher is deathly ill—as I read the day-by- day worsening of his condition, fearing, as she does, that he will die and reading her lament that she does not want to live if he goes, I fall into pain and sorrow. As if I am losing someone I cannot bear to lose. The sense of loss lingers through the day.

And these feelings of loss are combined with less and less tolerance for anything less than real—real conversations and real meetings. I am bearing the tension of these pulls, of these equal agonies.

I am finding the genuine inner space to be with the quick changes of heart, feelings, and thoughts, to neither run away nor get lost in the usual story line—leaving the gates open for the feelings and thoughts as they really are. I am seeing, more and more clearly, the pattern of needing real connection—and not giving it a story or letting my mind make use of it: "Settle for any kind of connection because I will die if I do not have any connection at all."

And I am being more honest with myself when I am feeling terrible and lonely. I am reaching out to make real connections . . . I want to have authentic connections and I am more willing to see how I blame the other person when I am dissatisfied with the connection . . . the temptation is to make up a story or believe my mind saying, "the other person is the problem—if only they were XYZ, then I wouldn't feel this way . . ."

Reach out and reach down—down into the silence, peace, and well-being that lives and breathes.

And watch as this practice, this happening over and over, with more and more awareness, ease, and lack of thought, grows. It seems important to watch, since it is so conditioned—notice the falls, the pain, the upset, and anger.

I am more comfortable with the reality and more uncomfortable when I have not been real or honest.

The sense of being separate keeps the feeling of needing, not getting a connection, and the pain of disconnect alive.

SEPTEMBER 8TH, 2012

I am thinking about the rapid shifts in me of light and dark, joy and pain, laughter and tears, love and anger, peace and irritation. I am remembering a vision from many years ago, when I ingested hallucinogens and came face to face with the all—the vivid awareness of the sameness of ecstasy and suffering. Now decades later I am reading Carl Jung's *The Red Book*: "But tears and laughter are one. Loving reaches up to Heaven and resisting reaches just as high. Unity, oneness, being in fullness and full realization of the Divine—being self-realized and whole, being at one in oneself."

The surrender I have intuited for a very long time—experiencing and accepting the totality of my experience and awareness. The letting go of what I perceive as a necessary protection—the sinking into something far greater and boundless. The nature of being in a mind, a brain that tells me I am unprotected and separate. The fears of that strike, that blow, that will hurt. The little-by-little of, with faith and trust, setting aside the mind's insistence that it is necessary to be angry, opposed to, protected in a thousand small and large ways.

The madness being the nature of us humans living inside a mind that tells us we are separate and therefore unsafe and alone, and acting as if that is true, experiencing slings and arrows which are further convincing us of our illusion.

Madness being the status quo—the way it is for all of us. Coming out of madness? Open to what is true, what is real—from the smallest perceptions to the ultimate reality of oneness.

And Jung again: "Thus I built a firm foundation. Through this I myself gained stability and duration and could withstand the fluctuations of the personal. Therefore the immortal in me is saved."

This is where faith and trust come in. Given that so much of my present experience is one of being at the whims of constantly changing emotions, then at times glimpses of a profound stillness and peace, and then falling into despair, discouragement, and self-hatred which most likely stems from deep disappointment and fear. Jung speaks to my long-standing intuition of needing to develop my ego, needing to build a firm foundation that can withstand these strong seesaws of emotions before being able to genuinely let go of the very same structure.

This is the second confirmation I am receiving that to be with the totality of my emotional experience, the light and the dark (Adya and Jung) is the matter of the moment and the practice of the presence.

PSYCHOLOGY AND SPIRITUALITY—MATTER AND SPIRIT—
TOWARDS A MARRIAGE
SEPTEMBER 14TH, 2012

Adyashanti: "Everyone is looking for intimacy, closeness, a sense of union with their own existence or with God, or whatever their concept of higher reality is. All this yearning actually comes from our longing for closeness, intimacy, and true union."

Donald Winnicott, a pediatrician, turned psychoanalyst: "The central issue for the baby is a connection with mother. We are wired with a desire and a longing to be held and merged with the environment of the mother, or mother figure, the merging that allows us to come into being, into existence.

"As adults, in the rarified experience of therapy we can find a close, intimate relationship between two people. This relationship reveals this early and deep yearning and longing, this looking for deepest sense of self. "

Adyashanti: "If we have no stillness within ourselves, life can be confusing, threatening, and completely nonsensical. This confusion has nothing to do with life; rather, it has to do with our conflict with life."

From psychoanalysis we see that we create a defense system to protect us from what we perceive to be dangerous, threatening, and scary. The reaction, the confusion is often in our minds as is the craziness. When we are little, when we are babies, we are defenseless and vulnerable. We arm ourselves against this dependency and live within this structure for the rest of our lives, if unexamined. The confusion, threat, and craziness within the minds of the human being, within the defense structure built to "protect" distorts our perception—we often perceive the world through the distortion of that lens, robbing us of clarity.

Or, to say it in another, more poetic way:

"The hearts of small children are delicate organs. A cruel beginning in this world can twist them into curious shapes. The heart of a hurt child can shrink so that forever afterward it is hard and pitted as the seed of a peach. Or again, the heart of such a child may fester and swell until it is a misery to carry within the body, easily chafed and hurt by the most ordinary things."

CARSON MCCULLERS
The Ballad of the Sad Cafe

Adyashanti: "When we continually judge and evaluate, we separate from what's happening. We feel a certain distance from our experience, because now we have become the evaluator of the moment and we're no longer in unity with the flow of existence and life."

Psychoanalysis: "Be with what is happening in the room. Be with the experience of the moment—not to get lost in figuring out, reporting, analyzing of, or even understanding of. This is the power of the full experience of the moment-to-moment encounter, in self and with each other, in the room."

SEPTEMBER 21ST, 2012

The cradle of life is the stillness underneath.

The dance of opening and closing. The dance of being in harmony and peace with what is, no matter what the it is, and the at-any-moment I can shut right down and close off. The mere practice of letting go, staying with whatever is happening long enough to naturally open-up again, is growing something inside me. The building up of faith and trust in the divine presence is allowing the process to stay alive and dynamic.

Life is opening—a stretch of fluidity and joy. I experience less and less fear, I have a sense of well-being and resolution no matter what. I have a preference for what feels good over what feels bad, and yet I feel more and more open to what is appearing on each block I am walking, and each moment I experience.

I am more aware of contractions as they occur.

GLIMPSES AND INSINUATIONS

I feel as if I am living in two worlds—the world of the mind and human interactions, and the world of a slow but steady relationship with a greater reality. I had a conversation today about politics and found myself able to articulate what I think is my relationship to life in general. To the fullest I am able in any given moment, I am engaged in daily life, relationships, and thoughts. I noticed I found it easy to enter the political conversation and be genuinely interested and engaged. I noticed a spontaneity that is new for me, or at least not very familiar.

At the same time, I am aware of feeling less and less caught up in anything that is not truly real.

In the back of my mind always is the wish and wondering about full residence in God. I have the feeling that a relationship with God is consistently deepening but I am hard pressed to put a lot of words to it. What I am aware of is the fluidity of everything that is happening in life, including moods and thoughts. Being able to recognize, admit, and accept whatever is happening.

I turn to *Daughter of Fire*, "Peace was mine. Sweetest peace, and I touched just the fringe of the most unbelievable happiness. . . . just a little of it. There was no end of it, and one day it will be mine . . . mine forever."

In my heart of hearts this is what I want to turn myself over to.

Continuing with *Daughter of Fire*, ". . . I woke up with the idea that such is my desire for Him that I will accept anything? Or was it the result of days, months of longing? Old girl, do you know? Whispers my heart . . . yes, I know. Have you any words left for gratitude? No, I have none . . . And so it came that the suffering of the sacrifice became gratitude and joy. The suffering was the fire, the sacrificial fire."

Oh my, oh my. Accept all as sacrificial fire. May it be so.

SEPTEMBER 23RD, 2012

I naturally fall into a deep place to speak directly to the divine. Offering myself, feeling a powerful connection. Remembering the years of prayer: "Thy will be done and may I be and know love."

I read in *Daughter of Fire* her experience of ecstasy and loneliness. She is immersed, totally immersed in a spiritual environment, being guided and influenced daily by her guru.

I am living in the world—influenced by teachers and awakened souls. I resonate deeply when she writes about the sorrow of loneliness, the aloneness of being left out of her guru's attention or circle, while others make merry. She has little choice in the matter.

I could keep myself busy; I could make sure I have company for most of the time. But I don't. I suffer the pain of loneliness, feel the pleasure of living a full life—not getting stopped or pummeled by the dark holes of depression. I have a sense of doing just what I need to be doing.

Daughter of Fire: "A crazy thing this love: the incredible thing . . . could it be called a spiritual life? If it is, what do you know of it . . . What do you know of the pain of it? 'And the glory of it' said the heart softly. . . So incongruous, so strange, so out of the usual from the point of view of the world . . . and to explain it? How can one? Who will believe it?"

And . . .

"It is pride. You think yourself better than the others and you hate them.

"It will go away. Things are done slowly. . . . When does Gold Ore become pure Gold? When it is put through a process of fire. So the human being during the training becomes as pure as God through suffering. It is the burning away of the dross. I told you that Suffering has a great redeeming quality. Like a drop of water falling on the desert sand is sucked up immediately, so we have to be: nothing and nowhere . . . we must disappear."

Being nothing and nowhere: a state to cultivate and devote to through surrender!

And so, life continues and what I am involved in shows clearly and remains mysterious.

Irina and I have come through this human condition differently and therefore appear to have different perspectives on suffering. I think we bring our own experiences to the surrender process—to the universality of it—she seems to have brought the Christian understanding of redemption—being saved from error or evil.

For me, suffering was a burr under my saddle—poking me over and over, to look under and around for what life was all about. And my predominant interpretation of believing myself separate was one of feeling alone and inferior; hers appeared to have gone in the direction of pride and superiority. Both are equally false interpretations of who we are.

SEPTEMBER 25TH, 2012

In real life, one is sometimes in sync with others and sometimes not. Sometimes the out of sync is temporary and other times it is permanent. I sense a transition in my life at this time. I am not as deeply emotional as I was during analysis, and I appear to have a somewhat clearer view of the human mind. A family member is convinced she is being taken advantage of financially. She believes this to her core and is able to make a very strong case for this being so. And yet, there is no factual evidence of this; it is doubtful this is real. Our minds can be, and usually are, profoundly convincing, leading us to truly believe whatever we are thinking. I am seeing through this madness now of the mind's flimsy constructs that we base our lives on.

My relationships are also changing. In so many cases we have a history of unconscious patterns set up between us. "I cannot be completely honest with you" (cannot hurt your feelings). "I will need you, for your sake" (so you will feel needed and good about yourself), or "I will pretend to be what I am not so you will like me."

My relationships are changing and I am mourning—mourning the difference and the loss, not reacting but navigating. I am navigating fear, sadness, and the unknown. I am responding to real life rather than the mind's constructs.

OCTOBER 2ND, 2012

Nothing in particular has happened and yet, I am aware of feeling an achy, full-body dull pain of separation. It is the pain of feeling separate and alone. I miss something, some connection; I am keenly aware of a heartbreaking yearning, a longing for something I cannot name—a unity, oneness, an intimacy. I am torn between knowing this is temporary and feeling the direct impact of it.

OCTOBER 5TH, 2012

I went to Dorothy Hunt's satsang (a local spiritual teacher), and during the meditation I felt the usual opening. In my mind's eye I saw an image of a large, colorful parrot.

Before Dorothy began her talk she invited a visitor from New York, M., to come and read some poetry. She read a Rumi poem and then a second poem by a woman I had never heard of before— someone from Norway or Sweden who now lives in southern Utah. The poem was very powerful, full of wildness and images. About a third way through, M. read the lines of a tree branch holding a wild colorful parrot. Had I intuited the parrot?

I loved the satsang. Again I felt an expanded opening— and by now I am recognizing and familiar with so many pointers—truths I have known. Reality includes everything. Nothing can be or is left outside of reality. Wholeness is inclusive, and we are whole.

I drove M. to her hotel and our conversation in the car touched on her experiences with awakening and her long-standing relationships with Adyashanti (Adya), Eckhart Tolle, Dorothy Hunt, and others. Our conversation was *manna*—a place where I was open with my experiences and where both of us could be and were present with each other.

OCTOBER 6TH, 2012

If you want the truth, the truth wants you.

Longing, at the human dimension, shows up as an agony for another human being to know, see, and be with me, and cannot help but end up in disappointment. The deeper longing, the longing for the very essence of being is calling us, rendering the yearning in us—the siren call of the soul—wake up to oneness.

> *"Those who love always cry—where there is deep love
> there is always separation."*
>
> IRINA TWEEDIE
> *Daughter of Fire*

Here is a paradox: essentially there is no separation; everything is one. And, in this worldly dimension we see and live with an apparent separation. I am here and you are there. It is within this apparent separation that we humans can, and do experience the deep longing for our natural selves, for love itself. It takes the separation, the reflection of something "out there" to stir the longing, the desire, and the call to love. Hence, as Tweedie comments, "where there is deep love there is separation."

OCTOBER 7TH, 2012

Carl Jung's *The Red Book*:

"The core of the individual is a mystery of life, which dies when it is 'grasped.'"

And . . . "one does not live one's self; it lives itself."

Life is living me. Words that help convey a growing seed in me are showing themselves more and more. Showing up as a deepening acceptance of what is in each and every moment. An increasing faith in living moment to moment, a growing aware- ness and acceptance of not knowing what mystery prevails. Not getting caught into the particulars of this situation, this person's viewpoint, or even more closely to home, what I am feeling in any given moment. Letting life live me.

Jung says, "The integration or humanization of the self as has already been indicated, is initiated from the conscious side by making ourselves conscious of our egotistical aims, that means we give an account of our motives and try to form as objective a pic- ture as possible of our own being."

My experience in analysis was that of facing myself honestly, willing to feel humbled and crushed. It was excruciating at the time. Looking squarely into the mirror and seeing the depth and extent of egoism, that everything I did and said came from a place of self-preservation. I am remembering the three o'clock in the morning reckonings and watching the truth reveal itself clear as day, seeing how totally and absolutely I had been motivated to be loved and taken care of in just about every single act. This urge towards self-preservation eclipses the capacity to truly take in an- other human and/or other aspects of life. I see this reckoning, this painful but clear introspection, as a powerful seed that led to this degree of freedom I now experience.

Jung writes: "The service of the self is therefore divine service and the service of mankind. If I carry myself I relieve mankind of myself and heal my self from the God."

I feel a deep resonance to relieving mankind of myself. Seeing through all projections, living from the deepest knowing within, accepting all feelings as they come, knowing the feelings are telling me something about my inner state, recognizing whenever I think it is the other person who is to blame, or causing my feelings. There is a way of going through life from a deepening self-realization and reality, freeing anyone else from the weight of my own projections—seeing them as causing my upset or disharmony.

Tapping into a deeper clarity—one without judgments and illusions. Beginning to recognize truth and clarity when listening to others—hearing what is real and what is made-up. I am able to hear the truth when not covered by a veil of disappointment.

I heard a story today about dyeing fabric in India. They immerse the cloth in dye and put it into the sun to dry. When the color fades they dunk the cloth back into the dye and then back into the sun. The process is repeated over and over until the cloth retains its color and is no longer bleached by the sun.

I can relate. This fits my experience of being in peaceful silence and soaring happiness, feeling at one with whatever or whomever is present for a period of time and then plop, going off center. I am particularly susceptible to this slide when I am alone. Being alone brings up deep longing and the slide into feeling alone, apart from everyone and everything.

I am comforted from reading *Daughter of Fire* as she journeys through the longing for her guru and then finds moments of transcendence where she sits in the pure presence within.

I know in my cells the human experience of being an infant who has been left or dropped and being so susceptible to the deep emotions of that experience. Having the many-layered consciousness of missing a mother and longing for the divine. I know the feeling of looking outside for the smile, the welcome and the I-am-there-all-the-time impossibility at the human dimension, yet omnipresent in divine presence and love.

Developing this awareness and reality little by little—each time going through the anguish and agony of the human pain and coming out into a lighter and more joyful state, I am opening to trust and faith in the interconnectedness of life in a real way, imbuing the cloth with deepening dye.

* * *

Anything can be responded to well with a clear view. Nothing is responded to well with an unaware blindness to the longing and loss within. Given the human experience of being hurt, dropped, confused, betrayed, at some time in one's life, we are primed to know loss and longing and we, until we know better, are inclined to look for what is missing out there.

Knowing the longing is within and for the transcendent frees me from casting about for the problem and staying stuck in the loop of being oppressed, frightened, and believing it is personal. This allows me to see the world more as it is.

OCTOBER 20TH, 2012

I had a session with Jan today—

Relaxed
No effort
Rubbery form, melting into eternal space
Welcome, welcome
Mind/thoughts enter and heart flutters
As if to say not really-of-much-help
No need to bother
Ease of falling, sinking, giving way, and feeling
Surrounded by feathers—soft and holding—cradled
In the love and tenderness of eternal quiet
And vast stillness
Sleepy—signaling how long the holding on, working hard, figuring out
As exhaustion seeps out of my body
Letting go, falling in
Now, and now, and now.

And then . . .

Ode to Resistance:

Amazing
The power of holding myself against my "will"
The sheer exhaustion of. . . what?

Of holding on
Resistance—a thing unto itself

As I feel the impressions and bruising of chains and folly
A sense of hard metal—nails and crosshairs
        Straight-jacket and shrouds of thorns

Self-inflicted—wanting something other than truth
Feet stomping, fists flailing, temper tantrums

I want it to be different
I want it to be different

Held captive by own mind
Tied into knots

Resistance and its cronies
Tempting and cagey
Clouding every view

And claiming its truth

A sight to behold
A revelation to know

In the marrow of my bones

To know is to love
Love and accept
Resistance in its glory

Invited into all that is

* * *

One of life's largest lessons is that nothing stays the same. Nothing
stays "wonderful" forever. Some significant part of my desire for

awakening is to not feel the "lower" feelings and not live from my ego anymore. What does it mean to want the ultimate truth more than these ego-saving passing fancies?

Remember it is choice. You can choose where to live.

Choose truth. Let go of what isn't real and pretends to be.

CLIMB THE MOUNTAIN
NOVEMBER 3RD, 2012

I am approaching my seventieth birthday and am feeling a calling to seek the deepest source. I have wandered the globe, virtually, looking for where I need to go. I wonder about a mountain in Turkey, maybe Machu Picchu, and then get excited about joining the Dalai Lama at a stadium. But realizing I would be one of tens of thousands, seeing him as a tiny speck from a long distance, I finally come to the obvious conclusion: I could have personal time with Jan. I set up a personal retreat with her. I will fly to Vermont, spend a week in a nearby B&B, and meet with her for some time each day—for five whole days!

JANUARY 7TH, 2013

My senses are heightened as the plane flies over the country. I look out the window and experience a profound immediacy—the green, the mountains, the sky, and the clouds—all right here. I am aware, seconds before it actually happens, that the cup of water perched on my sleeping seatmate's tray table is going to slip and potentially tip over. As I watch when it does begin to happen I pick it up before it spills.

I am sitting in the living room of a well-appointed home, with mounds of snow surrounding and covering the earth. It is all very quiet and I know, without having heard or seen anything that Jan has driven into the driveway.

I am full of excitement to see her walk from her car and rush to give her a hug. I am immediately struck by what I can only describe as an embrace that comes free from any defense, wall, obstruction, edge, or resistance. It is subtle and yet, I can say I have never experienced anything like it. This makes a strong impression on me.

We walked through the fire-warmed kitchen and hallway and climbed the stairs to the large room I was staying in and there, on two comfortable rockers and wide-armed chairs, with a wood-burning stove, we sat and "met" in person for the first time.

I cried when we sat down together—felt bursting . . .

I am in love.

Bits and pieces of our five days together . . .

Jan telling me story after story of people's awakenings—the man who sits under a tree and asks the sage who happens by how long until he, the man sitting under the tree, will awaken. The sage tells him it will be after many, many incarnations and the man screams and stomps his feet in protest.

And another man, also under a tree, asks the same sage when he will awaken. "See the leaves on this tree?" the sage asks. "It will be as many years as every leaf on the tree." The man laughs and says, "oh, wonderful." And awakens in that moment.

Jan tells me that losing my self might feel like going mad.

I tell her the dreams I have while I am there. I tell her my fears, anxieties, and petty upsets.

She asks me about my attachments and I tell her I am attached to being loved and respected and I am embarrassed at the telling. She points to being with the chagrin.

I talk about losing a sense of self. Sitting in the chair as she looks at the birds or the windowsill, I feel lighter, not dense, not holding on, as something inside me loosens up in her presence.

"Did you hear or see the fly?" She asks me. It is buzzing at the frosted-over window.

"How quiet it is out there," I say as I look at the untouched hills of snow outside the window and enjoy the snow-covered branches of the forests surrounding us.

"It is just as quiet inside you," she says.

"I have a sense," I say, "I don't know if it is intuition or ego thought, a feeling that the membrane is thinning out and I feel a sense of tipping over."

"The ego will continue to drain away," she responds, "only one direction it will go."

It is our last visit—I hate for her to leave.

She senses my tug and sends me an email when she arrives back home, gently reminding me that this longing lives in the belief that we are separate.

She writes:

[Imagine we are still sitting there]

It's like, for a time, a person needs to have a kind of "relation-ship" with it, to yearn for it, to be "dependent" upon the outer form of it, to pray to it, study it. None of those particulars really matter very much (the ways we orient to it), they are all expressions of one thing, which is the impression that it is separate from me. But something in us needs to do that dance, for a time. Until we no longer do. To follow on with the dance metaphor, it takes two to tango until it no longer does. Which must be something like the sound of one hand clapping.

I remember Gurumayi telling us about a saint who prayed to the beloved to be made separate in order that the beloved be wor-ship-able. The experience of longing, of adoration, of teacher-and-taught, is so sweet.

Loving you,

Jan

I certainly feel into what she is saying but even more so experi-ence what it feels like to be reached out, this extra mile, this level of connectedness.

* * *

Dear Jan,

I can and I do imagine us still sitting there and weep with and from your love. Thank you, thank you, for being my dance partner until you are not. I am listening to Bentinho, reading Krishnamurti, and feeling the immensity and awe of being able to know.

With deep love and gratitude,
Beth

JANUARY 13TH, 2013

First day home, I sense that something inside is emptying, draining.

Dear Jan,
If I may, I would like to share with you some snapshots from the past few days:
When I first came home I had a sensation of something draining out of me.
I listened to Norio's interview. And when he mentioned the word sorrow a dam seemed to break and I wept.
My head has been full of thoughts of my close relationships. I do not feel any resistance to the thoughts. I am hanging out with them passing in and out—assuming if I need to know something it will reveal itself.
I listened to your video on a *Normal Life* and experienced a gushing love over and over—being happy to see your picture and listen to your voice.
I listened to your *Normal Life* and *Daffodil* videos many times, and watched your satsang as well.
My head is full of my relationships. I let it be—I don't try to understand or get rid of anything.
I watched Bentinho and find a confirmation of increasing sensitivity and vibrations. I find his explanation of three freedoms very helpful and resonant in some deep place.
I am staying cloistered—other than work, keeping quiet—I have not had any conversations about my week with you.
I am reading Krishnamurti and getting a tiny sense of something ineffable and beyond knowing—and yet, its need to be reflected.
I read a couple of your blogs—the word grief popped out and another dam burst—I felt deep sorrow and longing—it felt relieving to be in it.
I spontaneously laugh when I see my crazy ideas and notions of what I think I am.

I realize my relationships are a mirror for my insanity or perhaps we reflect insanity to each other. This realization also brought relief.

Last evening I watched a satsang with Adyashanti from 2004. I fell into his eyes.

I had a penetrating realization that the whole self is unreal and know I did not realize the totality before. This was stunning.

I experienced a slow and peaceful disappearance of self.

I experience being silence—a full and yet, empty, velvet quiet.

This morning I experience a desire to cling to last night and it drops away.

With deep love, laughter and gratitude,
Beth

JANUARY 14TH, 2013

Smiling, laughing with you. Yum. Lovely to hear it all. Thank you for telling me.

Love to you . . .
Jan

JANUARY 26TH, 2013

Dear Jan,

Last night I dreamt that I was coming to Vermont to be with you again, leaving this Saturday. (Don't I wish!) I was surprised to learn that I would be taking a slightly different route this time; glad I was paying attention, but still ending up with you.

Being with you is taking a different route—
Beth

JANUARY 28TH, 2013

Hi, dear Beth.

I look forward to our next encounter.

Love,
Jan

FEBRUARY 2ND, 2012

Dear Jan,

It is late at night here and something in me is alert and very alive as a slow realization dawns—there is a gradual awakening happening inside me—gradual and subtle enough to be unrecognized—and yet, the way I have known myself is seeping out of me as flour from an un-seamed bag. And a steady stream of awareness and life is filling every crevice—showing up one moment as absorbing ecstasy, another moment a flood of tears, and yet another moment complete silence. Thoughts come and go, able to signal slight concern but have fewer places to root.

There is an edge, not wanting to engage in any unnecessary conversations—an edge that sounds a worry—and then a deeper rest into the unknown and uncertainty. Which brings such peace and happiness.

I rest here for now, with a deep reverence—the divine/love/ God I have intuited all my life is real and fills me with gratitude.

With much love to you, Jan.

Beth

FEBRUARY 3RD, 2013

So much love to you, dear Beth.

Jan

FEBRUARY 3RD, 2013

Good morning Jan,

I meant to include this in last evening's email but forgot: last week while sleeping I had a number of orgasms that were non-manipulated (solely from inside) and completely spontaneous. They traveled up, with tremendous full sense, to and through my solar plexus and into my heart.

I walked around that day in complete ecstasy—laughing to myself all day.

Quite delightful!

Lots of love,
Beth

FEBRUARY 24TH, 2013

Dearest Jan,

I spent the day yesterday with Adya in a retreat—sat grateful and moved when he spoke of the experience of being moved into a transcendent state and having to be in the world the very next moment, and also of the months to years it can take for the body to catch up and be able to adjust to the surges of consciousness.

I am keenly aware of these "getting used to's." My life is very quiet; in an organic way I have set up a cloistered world, going to work and class and having very few conversations with friends. I read Krishnamurti, Alice Gardner, and the *Daughter of Fire*. I listen to you, Adya, Eckhart, and various interviews on *BATGAP*.

I walk a lot in the Presidio, previously a military base, a magnificent forest of trees, rolling hills, flowers, and a view of the bay a couple of blocks from my apartment. The light in there is magnificent; one day I was wandering back home after sitting for a while overlooking the bay, when I was stopped in my tracks by the light on a completely brown, dead tree. It was luminous and filled me to overflowing.

I feel a little less bumbling in navigating the everyday world and life, thanks to a deepening ability to live moment by moment. I am aware of thoughts that are not real and watch as I get caught into the worry that they are. I appreciate the ordinariness of living within the practice of not resisting. And I get to practice non-resistance a lot! To tell the truth, I do have trouble when people in my life are defended or terribly unaware. This is no big surprise to me and probably not to you either.

Much love,
Beth

FEBRUARY 26TH, 2013

Hi Beth,

It's always so good to hear from you. Many has been the time, in recent weeks, when I'd have liked to linger over a meandering email to you. I've just been holding on by my fingernails, unable along the way to get to many things I would like to . . .

It's very white here now. So beautiful.

In the times when I've felt impatient with others' unconsciousness, or just ached that they could know how unnecessary their self-caused suffering is, all I've had to do is remember that it wasn't always so obvious to me either, and then there is a flood of acceptance into what-is. And then, there's something about how simply accepting a person as-is is a much more potent "environment" for "communicating" where you are, than is noticing the difference between you and them, or wishing they were other than they are. The whole problem is the impression that I am here and you are there, as if we are separate. Anything awareness can do to puncture that enduring illusion is a blessing. Meanwhile, when those times come, just turning and looking at the inner-whatever will disappear it . . .

Love to you,

Jan

FEBRUARY 27TH, 2013

Dear Jan,

Who knew? Who knew what was lurking in the shadows? Thank you for picking up on the more hidden piece of what I wrote to you.

It began with a strong pain in my heart as I felt the judgment and intolerance.

And I sat in it.

And sat, and sat.

Realizing/seeing the visceral sense of being locked inside a prison of my own mind—this actually caused a shudder in my whole system—And I sat some more.

Then I remembered a dream of being with a very deformed baby—grotesque limbs with no muscle mass—flopping on the bed and un-contained. I felt revulsion and wanted to leave but somehow needed to stay even though I didn't want to. I half-heartedly rubbed the baby's arm with my hand.

And then I remembered hearing that the "easy" stuff drains out first, the harder stuff is much more difficult to let go of. Amen to that.

And then I knew the state of self-involvement, defensiveness, separateness intensely and how much I either was afraid to or didn't want to let it go.

And then I remembered love. And now, this moment, I feel freer and lighter, more naturally related.

I send you lots of love,

Beth

MARCH 1ST, 2013

Dear Jan,

There is something visceral about the ego dying. I am having two experiences, one with a patient and another with a friend, where in order to genuinely love, something inside that protests is let go, has to leave—and I begin to see/feel/know that love is not abstract but instead burns away all that is in the way. In a gritty, in the body, every time being true to it kind of way.

Alice Gardner writes that at one point she wondered, sitting/being with others, who was feeling pain, or anger, or sadness? She did not know the difference between herself and the other person. I am keenly aware of that experience; in fact, it is the hallmark of the days in my office and conversations with my friends. And I wonder, is oneness unfolding and opening up, little by little, slowly but surely? The ego dying as something in me allows self-interest to go by the wayside and a more genuine feeling of empathy and kindness moves in? Death by death by death. I remember you saying to me, "who knows, this might be the last death."

This feels like a natural process that is having its way inside and as I watch and experience I wonder is this the death of separation (the illusion of separation) and birthing of oneness? I hold the question lightly as I live inside the birth pains.

I feel fortunate to have had a lot of training in self-inquiry and am able and willing to dive deeply into the ground of being/depths of the ocean, and from there know the folly of the protest as well as the respect for how it came about. From this "root" place the feelings and the letting go are more real/embodied—not an idea or thought. Much love to you,

Beth

MARCH 3RD, 2013

Daughter of Fire—

"Watching his family, I wondered why they seem so huge and noisy—I don't mean physical bodies . . . He is not at all like that, though he is also from a physically dense family. . . Suddenly I understood the why of it. . . they all carry their big selves with them, wear it like a garment. He has no self, and I try to get rid of mine. Because I am in the process of discarding mine, being so conscious of it, that's why they seem so huge to me, so noisy. . . All at once many things become clear; this is the focal point to keep in mind when the conflict arises, and probably in the near future many conflicts will arise, so I had better keep in mind that the reason for disturbance and suffering lies in the fact of being too conscious of something I am already discarding."

I am familiar with this dynamic of being annoyed, irritated, or bothered by someone's behavior or characteristic, and shortly after being triggered by this in the other person, that very trait shows up in me. It often feels as if, just as something is coming to the surface, but still hidden, I begin to notice it in others. And the noticing it in others is just what is needed for the unconscious behavior or characteristic to reveal itself.

MARCH 7TH, 2013

Dream:

I realize I know the music already and am made aware that I now have the fingering (literally, three fingers on left hand and all five on right) to play the music on the piano and need to keep practicing.

I woke up deeply happy. When I went out into the world I felt ungrounded but as the day progressed I found myself intensely, viscerally feeling each conversation and each person I encountered.

I feel strange. Emptied out. Slightly disoriented. And yet able to focus. All sorts of energy sensations. Aware and detached at the same time. Unfamiliar and not rattled.

Sometime today I thought, *oh, maybe I am losing control* (perceived control-tight vigilance). And how soft and kind and gentle it is.

MARCH 9TH, 2013

What am I seeing? The experience yesterday was of intense feeling of whatever environment I was in. In supervision (for work), I keenly felt the man J. told me about (scarred from sulfuric acid). I was the man and I felt the burn of the sulfuric acid. By the time I left J's office my body, including my head, was ringing and full of strong and powerful sensations.

Driving in traffic I felt anxious and stressed.

At dinner I felt confined by the smallness of my ego/mind, and felt jarred by my friend's need/insistence of trying to remember every detail, no matter what conversation we were having.

At times I feel and know the emptying of what I would call my sense of self. At times, like in J's office, it feels clear that I am experiencing another person's being. And at other times, like dinner with my friend, I am painfully aware of the insistence of my ego.

I am beginning to come into contact with the interconnectedness of everything and everyone. I am sensing its permeability. And I am, in moments, caught in the net of interpretation—my friend (and by clear extension, me) should not be trying to remember every detail, should not be controlling or fearful. It is the should-not that creates the constriction, the smallness, the jarring.

Daughter of Fire: "This diary spans five years, making up an amazing record of spiritual transformation . . . the agonies, the resistance, the long and frightening bouts with the purifying fires of Kundalini, the perseverance, the movement towards surrender, the longing, and finally the all-consuming love."

From a psychological viewpoint the diary maps the process of ego dissolution, gradually unveiling the openness and love that reside beneath the surface of personality.

Amen.

MARCH 12TH, 2013

I live inside the prayer refrain: "Thy Will Be Done."

With an eye or whatever on letting go completely.

MARCH 14TH, 2013

"Invited residence."

A line in a poem I wrote a bit ago comes to me again. I reread the line!

... and now reading *Krishnamurti's Notebook*.

"Where the self ends, with all its secret and open intrigues, its compulsive urges and demands, its joys and sorrows, there begins a movement of life that is beyond time and its bondage."

I invite residence—residence beyond time and its bondage.

I send out a prayer into the universe—

"Thy Will Be Done."

MARCH 18TH, 2013

Hello dear Jan,

It is Monday morning and I have a bit more leisure before heading off to see my patients. Since I have been "talking" with you (in my head) for days now it made sense to "speak out loud." I hope you are well—how is the recording of your book coming along? And I send my best to your family as well—four legged as well as two.

I saw your interview with Rick Archer and was struck by you saying that by the time you pray something out loud something has aligned long before. I got quivers when you said that and was aware of the latest prayer refrain of "Thy Will Be Done" that was filling my life.

A couple of days later I awoke feeling very disoriented and spacey—having no firm location of the "me" I am accustomed to. Since it was Tuesday I drove an hour away for supervision—the drive being an unusually beautiful one for highway driving. The highway cuts through green hills, forests of trees, and along bodies of water. There were two realities: one I was aware of being focused on driving; I watched the road, other cars and my maneuvering of my car, and in another reality, I was aware of the full sensation of moving, moving, and there being no time. Only sensation. At one moment, I looked over at the hills and felt the sensation of the wet, moist, dark, rich earth. I was the earth. Even the taste . . . This was a much bigger reality/experience than I have words to describe.

I was able to have a mini-conversation with my supervisor (she is interested in spirituality) and by the time I left her office I thought every circuit, physically, in my body was going to burst. By now, driving home, it felt as if I needed to get grounded so I went swimming, which did ground me; who knows if that was what was really needed.

By the time I went to class that evening I was still filled with extraordinary energy. And my mind/ego took over; somehow feeling uncomfortable/threatened by the confines of the conversation of my fellow students and the class material, and I sat in the strong currents of discomfort—aware and amazed at what can go on and be held in awareness. By the way, a couple of weekends ago I went to my friend's anniversary party with 125 guests, most of whom I knew. I was very apprehensive about going since my experience coming home from Vermont is that I get flummoxed in social and/or everyday situations. I spent the day of the party sitting in nature, quietly praying and surrendering. It felt important to be at the party in an open and loving way and it showed up just like that. Yay! There does seem to be movement in being with people, in a real way. So Tuesday evening, back in class, shows up as more room and opportunity for practice—from moment to moment.

All in all, I sense a natural unfolding process.

Yesterday, I cleaned the blinds in my apartment and was aware of how quiet my mind was and how my body alerted me when it was time to rest. I continue to lead a quiet life; aware of truly being, and being single focused. Are you familiar with the teaching, "If Thine Eye Be Single, Thy Whole Body Will Be Filled With Light?" I don't know where it comes from but it has been humming inside me—making great sense of surrendering fully and whole-heartedly to the ultimate reality of the divine.

Well, I do need to get dressed and to my office. As always, I send my deepest love and appreciation to you.

Beth

MARCH 19TH, 2013

Beth,

It's so good to be dipped into these awareness unfoldings. Notwithstanding the limitations of language, you are very adept at portraying these subtle and powerful things.

About this: "And my mind/ego took over; somehow feeling uncomfortable/threatened by the confines of the conversation of my fellow students and the class material, and I sat in the strong currents of discomfort—aware and amazed at what can go on and be held in awareness."

I get the point you're trying (I think) to make, that latter part about what can be held in awareness. And it also makes me want to reflect something. Just point to something to look at, play with. Disliking a situation (social, constricted, whatever) isn't automatically egoic. I wonder if there might be times when you feel yourself leaning away from something (having a preference for otherwise) when you assume that even subtle recoiling must be ego-driven.

One thing you're learning is how to take care of yourself. How to be in the world, in familiar situations. How to drive, for instance, and experience the passing terrain the way you so deliciously portray below, but also keep from merging with a tree. There's an attuning of degrees of consciousness that's going on here, and it's the same in social situations. How big to let yourself be, how small (with focused-in attention) a given situation asks you to be.

111

There's lots of learning about being with people, the kinds of situations you welcome and don't. I'm just suggesting you not jump to assumptions about what's going on. It might just be an experience giving you data that's of use. How you learn to tell, to recognize for what it is, when preference is operating. Of course a lot happens prior to preference. Preference is how you (the mind, I suppose) interpret the body's warming toward or leaning away from something. Anyhow, words are starting to get to be too much here, but I think I've said enough.

Love,

Jan

NAVIGATING RELATIONSHIPS

Since returning from Vermont I feel a sense of continual confusion and unrest about my long-standing friendships and relationships. I speak with Jan about this on a regular basis—giving her example after example of the challenges I am facing, how and when I find myself getting defensive and confused. I tell her about the guilt I feel for no longer being interested in the ways we have always related or not wanting to stay in friendships even though they have lasted a very long time. ("Did you really expect to go through such a large shift and not have it impact your relationships?" She asks me with her tongue planted firmly in her cheek.)

Dear Jan,

I had a dream a few nights ago where *I am with some friends and dozens and dozens of other people. They are all in a very active/busy state and are going to the "fair." I become aware I am not going to join them—register a deep sadness and then see the trees and ocean. I see myself sitting in the crook of one of the trees and register a deep happiness.*

When I woke from the dream I thought about the word fair, being righteous and civic minded. Living in the world of separation and a moralistic right and wrong—fair.

The dream is reflecting a movement I am experiencing with many relationships and friendships (as you and I have touched upon over and over). It is also reflecting the movement from my own internal busy state (mind chatter), and the life of duality (fair) is being reflected in this dream . . . the movement from living from there into living inside the natural state of expansion and being. Not that it isn't sad to say goodbye! Externally and internally!

I have felt a longing for a relationship/connection/love "out there" for most of my life and it has dawned on me today that since returning from my time with you, the longing is gone and I reside in a deep abiding presence that surpasses anything I could have ever imagined.

With much love and appreciation, thank you for listening. It helped to put all this into words.

Beth

APRIL 13TH, 2013

I reread a few paragraphs of what I have written in the past and was struck by the omnipresence of longing and wishing for connectedness with a person out there. What is so striking about this is that the longing is pretty much, if not altogether, gone. The deep connection with life and presence is alive and has settled the longing and the tendency to be looking outside. I am content and held in a vastness of love that has shown itself over and over since returning from Vermont. Such awe and gratitude!

Subject: Sigh
Dear Jan,

I am just returning home dragging my very tired body around after being awake much of last night—feeling pretty badly. I am tossed about by thoughts and feelings of sorrow and guilt, watching as I try to figure a way out of this inner conflict and scary fallout, and watching as I laugh at the folly of control. I do appear to be able to stay aware, including watching the ways I go unconscious and noticing deep patterns . . . I feel horrible and guilty and then I remember I have no idea how things will unfold and I am allowing myself to get all worked up over a belief and churned up worry. Then I see, many times, the impulse to apologize for "leaving" and in that I can see a strong pattern that I have acted upon over and over throughout my life. I have been aware before of the lengths I will go to be "taken care of" and I watch as I worry that I will get sick or infirm, and will have no one there. Then I try on for size the conversations and relationships I know well and I know I cannot and do not want to continue in that unconscious vein.

I think you get the picture.

I am going on faith and a prayer—and you, and other awakened people, saying this is a natural part of the process of cleaning house of unconsciousness that shows up after some form of awakening.

I am not unfamiliar with this mind-field terrain at all—what does seem different is the awareness of the state. Last night when I couldn't sleep I got up and re-read your email for the umpteenth time and watched Adya talking about letting go. I instinctively know there is a letting go involved and what bubbled up from deep inside was settling into love and falling into that.

I had had a dream a couple of nights ago, *I watched a native American man demonstrate how to fall off a ledge and be held in such a way that his fall was natural, without tension, and his landing soft. I wanted to know more about this man and when I looked on a map to see where he was I saw he was from a town I hadn't heard of but it was right outside a town very close by. Close but not familiar.*

Writing this out to you has lifted something in me. My body is achy and tired, but my spirit and heart are lighter. So I think I will stop here for now. And go make some homemade lentil soup.

With much love and gratitude,
Beth

APRIL 16TH, 2013

Good morning, dear heart.

This image comes to me, as I sit with what you're experiencing. The pain comes (only) when you hold yourself—or try to—at a distance from what's happening, what you're feeling. You literally are what you're experiencing (this is always the case, when we aren't trying to resist . . . and in that case, we are resistance). Wishing this were all otherwise, trying to find your way out of it, is trying to put "you" at a distance from it . . . which is the source of the pain. It is playing itself out within all the boundaries of what you are. Life is at play within you, and to the extent that you can simply allow that to be, without trying to sort it all out, you will be more at peace in the unknowing.

So much of what is happening, it seems, is in response to the historical relationship(s). It's like paying the piper backwards, or something. (Well, I guess the piper only ever gets paid for something that occurred before now.) Just saying that part of why this is such a big thing, and the discomfort so wild, has to do with the recognition of long-term patterns, living not quite honestly, or living from egoic motivation in relationship, which is very far from love. So painful to have to be with all of that—all at once, as it were. The accumulation of it all.

I love you so. Don't wish it will be over. Don't wish you could get out of it. Just be like that guy falling backwards into it, no idea how far down the landing place is.

Jan

With That Moon Language

"Admit something:
Everyone you see, you say to them, 'Love me.'

Of course you do not do this out loud, otherwise
Someone would call the cops.

Still, though, think about this, this great pull in us to connect.

Why not become the one who lives with a
full moon in each eye that is
always saying,

with that sweet moon language,
what every other eye in
this world is

> *dying to*
> *hear?"*

HAFIZ
Love Poems from God

APRIL 22ND, 2013

Dearest Jan,

Yes, I feel the flight intensely. Last night as I was falling asleep I became aware that, in all my life, I have not really loved anyone (my children and grandchildren being an exception). The bold truth, as I saw vividly, was all other relationships were out of need. And none out of desire or attraction. I saw how I used seduction to get what I wanted/needed. It is a sobering truth and even though when it came to me I felt a sense of relief for the big truth of the matter, I had another restless night telling me it is harder medicine to swallow than first blush.

I know that it couldn't have been any other way given how much was lacking but I also know there is freedom and release in facing and being with the pain, with compassion, no excuses, and, as you say, the accumulation of it all.

And I hear you—be with what is—be with what I am feeling and experiencing.

And there is grief. And guilt. And some self-pity.

And it is a lot.

Patterns, dishonesty, and egoic motivations—I am writing it out to allow it into my body.

And as I am writing this I have become aware of another distancing strategy—"Oh, goody, look at this. I get to do something courageous!" Taking me away from the pain.

May I fall into all that life is living in me.

I hope you know the life and love line you are providing.

Love to you,

Beth

APRIL 23RD, 2013

There is no end to your courage, Beth. Such willingness to be truthful, to get it all. You are seeing into the depth of frailty of a (every) human being. How vast our need. How willing we are to go to any lengths (including the deception of self and others) to get it. And a tender vastness surrounds your willingness to let it all reveal itself. Something tenderly ministering to you as you go through it all.

Loving you,

Jan

APRIL 24TH, 2013

Thank you Jan—so very much.

There is something deliciously full of wonder and freedom being with what is . . . I am under the weather today (from serious sleep deprivation, I am sure). I don't think there has been a week since January that I have not missed at least one night's sleep (and this past week, two) and it takes its toll.

I am aware that through all the states of being I have been in since being with you, the issue of relationships has been present. At times it was a thin thread, and at times thicker, and at times, like in the last couple of weeks, pretty demanding. I don't presume to understand it but find it helpful to "not wish or expect it to be different." I feel a lot of grief and I am aware that, being sick, I am even more susceptible and tender. I feel loss—deeply and intensely. And a lot of pain.

And yet . . . over the days in the wake of seeing the truth of my self-centeredness, I have found "myself" being awareness, looking at the human condition, mine and others, from a quiet, neutral, and peaceful field—where everything is simple and clear.

So muddle and clarity—and both are what they are. Many, many years ago I had a realization that made only a little sense to me at the time. It was that agony and ecstasy were the same. Not only does it now reside as a reality in me but I also have lately been remembering knowings and realizations throughout my life that I now see as glimpses into what is.

I just re-read your last email . . . And a tender vastness surrounds your willingness to let it all reveal itself. Something tenderly ministering to you as you go through it all. Having you remind me of this and point towards it helps enormously. Choosing life by dying death by death.

With deep gratitude,

Beth

MAY 28TH, 2013

I had a phone session with Jan yesterday—I am getting guidance and perspective so I can let go.

There seems to be a downloading of insight going on inside me.

Last night:

I sold my soul to belong.

I have been keenly aware of that insight many times in my life.

However, I don't need to belong anywhere, and I belong everywhere.

Truth of this.

I am feeling tense—I am not able to fall asleep.

I remember what it was like the night before, I felt a stark terror in an existential way and almost immediately my mind took me to the story of my early childhood.

As I look now I see that the terror is more immediate—I am right now, facing an abyss, and I appear to be willing to die or fall into it and feel whatever shows up.

Please help me die and let go—I cry out.

With this willingness, with this commitment I come face to face with the existential abyss that stirs terror in my heart . . . I know it is fear of death and my voice cries out again . . .

> *Help me*
> *I am completely willing even though I am scared*

I woke up feeling lighter . . .

"I came across something Osho said about Buddha, which I loved. Buddha said the first awakening is like entering the stream, you recognize oneness, and sixty percent of the mind is gone forever. You

cannot ever fall into the illusion again. Yet, then there are the other forty percent . . ."

RANI
Ordinary Buddhas
by Anatta Campbell

I entreat myself, write it down; write it out. Find the space around it . . .

The emptying out of a conditioned way of relating that is alive today, now.

The emptying out of relating out of need and fear.

Relating out of need and fear

Relating out of need

Relating out of fear

Relating without need and fear

Relating without need of the other person making me okay. That is profoundly real. And yet, I feel susceptible to rejection and not being loved.

Relating without fear—more trouble here—

What if

This dies

Dissolves

Evaporates

Right now my anxiety is strong. I watch it—I go about my business and watch it. There really is no need to give it a lot of attention. There is no real danger I need to be paying attention to. I remind myself, *don't ignore but don't indulge.*

My anxiety. It is hard to imagine being free of an anxiety that has been with me for most, if not all, of my life. It is like a second skin—and what is not known here, cannot be known here (from the conditioned mind) is how life, life itself, moves and generates responses, creative and affirming responses. From the conditioned mind it is impossible to know that letting go, letting go of fear and illusion, opens us to a truer and far reaching wellness. A well-being that navigates through this "person," a well-being that flows with everyday life and responds creatively and efficiently to every circumstance. It is like living with more engine power than can be even imagined from the limited scope of our small selves.

And I quote Rani again: (*Ordinary Buddhas*)

"[H]ere is somebody who knows at any given moment of the day and night what reality is, that all is one. Sometimes clouds drift by and create obscurity. I am no longer afraid of these clouds; they are welcome as the bliss experience.

When a cloud or storm arises then that part of the mind says, 'Hello, I want to be liberated. Set me free.'"

When a cloud or storm arises then that part of the mind says, "hello, I want to be liberated, set me free."

Hello—I want to be liberated. Set me free.

I want to be liberated. Set me free.

Rani again:

"Sometimes it's the questions, 'Who am I?' or 'Can I know that that is true?' I call these last few years a maturing into being. It is an ongoing humbling . . . I see that we all have homework to do after awakening. Yet it is not work and IT undoes itself, but it needs a little help. It needs the intention to say, 'Who am I?'"

MAY 26TH, 2013

I am listening to Adya's talk on the stages of awakening.

I can locate the glimpses of the different experiences I have had and am having:

The awakening of the mind—the blissful experience of the transcendent.

The awakening of the heart—the experience of oneness, no separation, intimacy.

Yes, to both.

The awakening of the gut—the full emptying of the ego/mind.

No—clearly no—as I watch my mind and ego's activities.

The edge of surrendering to death—I have a clear awareness of the vastness and no self—but not the experience, flesh, and blood reality lived in and through.

I know I am pure love and know the bind of human fear—

That being said, I seem to see it all from a very different perspective—I feel, experience, and am engaged in the energy of whatever is showing up . . . and at the same time it is apparent that it means nothing and so it passes.

* * *

And in this midst . . . last night "I" watched myself sleep and dream. A very curious experience—what is watching? What is not asleep?

I am thinking about faith and trust these days. I appear to be guided, there is something inside always present and alive—sometimes loud and sometimes so quiet. And now this presence is constant—even within the midst of fear and doubt—it seems to be lying immediately underneath. When a friend asks me if awakening is worth it—with one deep breath I am in the ocean of love and joy—right there for the tasting and touching.

JUNE 8TH, 2013

I reread a patch of this chronicle where I lament about how alone and lonely I feel. And realize that I no longer have even a whisper of those feelings—erased—evaporated—gone.

It is very nice to make note of it. Once again, I am aware of how quiet absence is—making it easy to miss, even though it is powerful and right there, breathing in and out all the time. All the noise (the hundreds of distractions I am used to living in and with) takes up all the space. If I was still feeling lonely and alone "I" would be strongly aware and picking at it like a splinter.

But the absence! The quiet restful breath that is omnipresent, profoundly holding everything and anything is always there. Amazing!

Being whole, undiminished, no matter what I feel, no matter what I have done, no matter what has been done to me.

* * *

Jan is coming out for a small retreat—there will be eight of us staying in two houses, being together in satsang and inquiry for three whole days. This came out of my time with her in January. My friends, who introduced me to Jan, are hosting the retreat at their beautiful home in Marin County. All of us are drawn to Jan's presence and it is clear that my being with her in Vermont has propelled something in me. We are all anticipating the privilege of sitting in her presence (and living together) for three days.

I am excited to see her again in person. I feel awestruck . . . like a giddy teenager.

I pick her up at the airport and feel shy. Not only shy, somewhat nervous. There is a sense of coming to the edge of something.

JULY 9TH, 2013

At the retreat we are surrounded by natural beauty—green hills, trees of varying sizes and shapes, birds soaring/gliding, fog coming in and out—

We are sharing meals, laughing a lot, and listening to each other and ourselves, deepening what we are aware of each time we meet.

And I jot down notes to myself:

What wants to be said/known
Tired body
Days of immense gratitude for the beloved
Rest—full rest—my god, how I long for that.
I feel tense, aches, and tiredness
Closeness to every person in the room
    So rare
  I feel love for everyone
Being in each moment
    Aware of tension/tightness
    Aware of longing to be free
Fully free
Protecting image

Self-concept
    Wanting to be seen in "good light"
Aware of that belief that I have to earn love
Not sleeping
    Be awake
Feel what it's like
    Feel the sheets
    Smell the air
    Listen to the sounds of the night
Don't wish it otherwise
Relax, rest in being awake
    Sounds easier said than done

JULY 11TH, 2013

We are sitting together in the beautiful living space, sharing sofas and soft chairs, giving voice to where we are internally.

Yesterday, hearing each person speak—and each person, each voice, sinking inside me with a steady yes-ness. I feel no resistance . . . none at all. It feels open, spacious, and I am aware of a sense of grace—sinking into every beloved being as they speak, and sinking deeper and deeper into an unending acceptance. It feels internal . . . like everyone and everything is internal.

Today—being each person as they came forward and spoke. Being them.

A resonance of complete accord

Not a merge—and yet nothing, nothing at all between us

Over and over again

As natural and unspectacular as breathing—oneness . . . at-one-ment

    We are all sitting together in silence . . . in meditation—

Feeling/sensations

Hearing Jan's voice

Feeling my heart break

My stomach sob

Sink into fear

There is an intense, visceral burning in my gut. My whole body heats up; I would swear I am feverish. The fire in my gut burns hotly, giving off the sensation of something being cleaned out, burnt away, physically and obviously—continuing and continuing. My eyes are closed and I am convinced this would be visible to anyone looking— meaning my skin would be bright red and flushed—it feels real . . . it feels manifest. I am physically uncomfortable and unresisting.

And a thought passes through me—*dear God, wouldn't it be wonderful to wake up here amidst and with these lovely people. Oh, to fall fully into awareness in good company!*

We end the retreat and say goodbye to each other. I am going to drive home to San Francisco. Jan is leaving the following day for Vermont. Before leaving I spend a luxurious amount of time saying goodbye to her, visiting, talking, and being together as the day and the retreat end. We sit in her room, as the light and sun lowers and talk about my childhood in a most natural way, even though we have not had this conversation before. Jan asks me about the sexual abuse and wonders, aloud, how a parent can hurt a child as my father did; how a mother could not know. I am aware of a compassionate human being, a woman, a woman I love dearly looking after my well-being, caring how it was for me. I am also aware of feeling compassion for my father, my mother, and myself, deep in my bones and viscerally understanding the depth of unconsciousness in us human beings. And how we hurt each other; my God, how much we hurt each other.

I say goodbye to Jan and go home for a good night sleep in my own bed.

JULY 12TH, 2013

The next morning, lazily, I am lying on the couch in my living room, feeling exhausted and empty, happily so. When it dawns . . . my God, just like that, it dawns. It happened. This being woke up to itself—it was gentle and quiet—and now, in the quiet space alone, it could be recognized.

I take a shower and realize I am going to shout this across the nation so Jan can hear. I remember Adya saying he didn't mention his realization to his teacher for many months. I cannot wait to announce it!

I walk down to Fillmore Street with my mouth agape. Here are the same stores, the same streets, the same trees, and pretty much the same people I typically see meandering the streets. And yet how profoundly, how irrevocably different everything looks. Awareness is looking, the filters are gone, the veil is evaporated, swept away, and awareness, presence is looking and seeing.

My God . . . so simple, so matter of fact, and yet, completely earth shattering.

JULY 12TH, 2013

To: Jan Frazier
Subject: Did you know?

Dearest Jan,
　　Welcome home—
　　Did you know? Could you tell? Did it show?
　　There are a hundred ways I can say it—or just a few
　　It happened
　　The gears radically shifted
　　The entire perspective is different
　　The switch flipped
　　The rocket left the atmosphere
　　Everything is different and everything is the same
　　I died and went to heaven
　　It was so gentle, soft, and tender as the membrane broke that I am only today aware of the magnitude of what took place yesterday. And at the same time the utter simplicity of it all—as if it has always been there, but isn't that what you and the others have been saying all along?

　　The thread, as it looks to me right now, in reflection, moved from the tender realization and willingness of complete surrender, being open hearted, through to the spontaneous no-separation between me and each and every person in the room, in a felt, real way, to the burning of all that was held in my gut, a cleansing fire—unfolding during days of unceasing being-ness, love, and presence—up to and through our deep being with each other last evening; and the cherry-on-top when you said I could imagine what being fully awake is like.

Every one of these moments beg to be opened up more fully—
As it reveals itself over time.
With so much love and gratitude,
Beth

JULY 13TH, 2013

Oh, dear love,

I am sitting here all tingly. I'm not surprised. Your eyes, my God. I think what I saw, felt, knew, was that—if it wouldn't happen for her, being as she is, then for whom? Which isn't to say I could ever reliably predict, etc. It's just a way of saying how I experienced multiple times (not just in Mill Valley but before) the utter surrender, willingness. And I felt so much love pouring, leaking out of you, in so many settings, with so many expressions. Some you may have been aware of, some maybe not. Who knows? Just saying there was a lot more going on, in the room where we sat together in the lowering darkness, "telling stories" (your history, etc.), than the surface thing that could have been filmed or caught by a recorder. I have been aware, in retrospect, of things "deliberately" done (by me, of course I really mean by whatever moves through "me"). Doing something in an outward way (like asking what happened in your youth) while knowing the exchange is not really "about that." Oh, I think not to go on about this just now. Just saying that I/it never rests. No missing of an opportunity, an opening. What looks like ordinary conversation, or just "doing stuff" together . . . what might seem random, or insignificant, trivial, just "practical stuff"—I am aware always that more is going on, and sometimes afterward, when the reflecting part of me turns on, I see it vividly and I marvel at it.

Give yourself as much alone time as you can. I know you have already been doing this. But don't "stress" yourself, if you can avoid it, with chores, social stuff, contact with the world that asks you to be a regular person. If any thought comes to you (will this last? What does something mean? What's next? Etc.), allow a great distance from the thought. Like you've just landed on a new planet where things like thoughts occur and it's a curiosity. Even if there is a pull toward the thought—to believe it, identify with it, think it's "your" thought—get enough distance from that too. If there is any fear of anything, let yourself collapse into it.

I wish I had thought to tell you this when we were together, and I was telling you about Anne (who always knew she would wake up, and then did). On the subject of fear: maybe I told you this when you were here in the winter. How after she woke up she had an episode of fear in the middle of the night, and how she dealt with that. I bet I did tell you. The point is that it did happen, and she knew enough to not freak out. To surrender utterly to it. And came out (literally) laughing. It's all laughable . . . so long as you don't pull away, start thinking "uh oh, what's wrong?"

I love you dearly, Beth. Whatever happens, remember Gandhi and his "Ram" with each bullet. It's not just God if it feels good.

Jan

JULY 12TH, 2013

Threading back a moment here to the day "after." To repeat myself a bit here with an emphasis on wanting to keep opening up the realization of realization: I am utterly spent, resting after our retreat—lying on my living room couch with my eyes closed. And I am hit with the realization—honestly, I feel shocked and giddy—my God, it happened. How could I have missed it and yet, the knowing is solid and without question even though "I" feel exactly the same. I lie there for some time somewhat breathless and amazed. I take a shower and think there is no way I can keep this quiet—I want to shout it loud enough for Jan to hear across the country.

I walk down to Fillmore Street and have the experience of every corner; every store, every tree, and each person looking exactly as they did "before" and yet . . . awareness itself is gazing upon everything and is everything. It is all the same! New eyes? No, new perspective . . . something is emptied out—what was looking out before is not there, like some cool breeze came along and wiped away all markings and form and can now see and be from a completely clear and empty perspective. It is wild and profoundly energizing.

* * *

Notes from right after . . .

TRADING PLACES

It began, throughout childhood and adulthood, with the whisper of the eternal and the prominence of the "little me" . . .

Several years ago, likely around the time of my first encounter with breast cancer and facing the possibility of dying . . .

Where the whisper of the eternal turned up the volume and "the little me" complained.

Where the whisper turned up the volume, stayed around longer and the crusty build-up of protections and conditioning began to be dislodged in all my organs.

And now the vastness took over and "the little me" is a whisper.

ONENESS IS NOT MERGING

I have had a long-held misconception that oneness would resemble what I understood merging into would be. Like I would "become" the other and experience life as they do . . . looking through another's eyes with the unconscious assumption of separation still prevailing; you are over there, I am here but I empathize with you—leading to a profound misconception of what it might mean to be unified. Empathy is real. It is a powerful connecter, allowing us to see each other, feel each other, and understand each other and allowing us to be seen. It can and does heal deep wounds. In its presence we humans feel safe.

The deeper and fuller truth though, the profundity of unity, of oneness is the visceral knowing of everything being awareness, vibrating emptiness—everything, at its essence is that and so all is one, all is connected with no beginning, no end, and simply is not separate—cannot be separate. There is no outside, there is no inside. There is no substantial, solid you, no substantial, solid me. "We" are temporary forms; we are temporary movement, rising out of emptiness, out of an infinite one—

Look deeply enough and you will find our common source—

* * *

JUST SIT THERE RIGHT NOW

"Just
sit there right now.
Don't do a thing. Just rest.

For your
separation from God
is the hardest work in this world.

Let me bring you trays of food and something
that you like to
drink.

You can use my soft words
as a cushion
for your
head."

HAFIZ
Love Poems from God

JULY 13TH, 2013

Watching the tree outside my window and feeling/being the movement as the wind whistles through the leaves and around the branches—feeling/being the swaying as the wind increases . . .

Awakened in the middle of the night—

Being infused with the vastness/the pure nothingness (no form) of the divine—as if something is watching as it soaks in through every cell in my body. It is immense and the experience is visceral. Every sense is attuned and the vastness is palpable. It is like being filled in by the ocean or the very atmosphere we breathe in and out.

Touchable.

The next night I awakened again. It is less intense than the night before but there is a surging of energy throughout my system. I have the feeling that the divine is taking up permanent residence and the body has to adjust and rearrange itself.

* * *

Dearest Jan,

Thank you from the bottom of my heart for your full and loving response to me. I was in a driveway in Sonoma (a friend had gathered ten women together to celebrate her seventieth birthday) when I saw your email and I stopped everything to read and savor each and every word and take in the deep love and connection that is filling me to overflowing . . . I love that you were tingly.

I am a rushing river charging with immense energy . . . not containable and yet when the traffic stopped short on the freeway for many, many miles, everything inside calmed and slowed down.

I am happiness and joy.

And so much love—and free; can you believe that? Completely free. I know you can.

I wrote to you Friday evening, before going to bed and before going up to Sonoma. I was awakened after a couple of hours of sleep with this happening: an infinite, formless, immense emptiness bubbling with life began to fill/spill into every pore of my being and as I watched/felt it, in complete awe, I became aware of a structure that somehow made clear that it was, up until that point, everything I had believed myself to be. I watched as it began to dissolve/evaporate/disappear into the energy. Just as the very last tiny bit was going to be subsumed something in me pulled away.

And saw/felt a "sentry" surrounding the fortress, lamenting the falsity of what was being experienced. I take it all with a grain of salt, seeing the thread of vigilance that was woven throughout our time together and being aware that our "random, insignificant, storytelling" is bringing something to consciousness that needs slow and comforting letting go, meaning keeping a fully open heart and allowing a needed death to take place.

The next night, sleeping in Sonoma, once again I am awakened after a couple of hours of sleep and feel an immense current of energy filling my body and somehow know that "I" am being rearranged; perhaps adjusting to the influx of greater awareness/consciousness.

The next couple of nights, as I lay in bed I become aware of how light my body feels—so, so light, so little matter. I think it is relaxed as never before!

My time with patients yesterday was fluid and remarkable in that there was very little thought and yet an intimate continuous conversation—in fact, more intimate and alive than ever before. In full harmony with wherever they are as it appears there really is no separation. One of my patients, who rarely lets me say anything, and needs desperately to be heard, stopped still whenever I said anything and all my patients mentioned how beautiful I looked in purple!

I am being a complete "chatty Cathy" as I go through these days. Many of the women at my friend's party were reading your book and I had several occasions to have one-on-one conversation with some of the women and I found myself telling them what was going on in me—as if I could do otherwise with so much love, energy, and joy spilling out of every pore. Then today I went to my consultant for work and "spilled the beans" to her as well.

And as I am being with you now . . . I want to tell you this, and then that, and then this some more. And here is the next thing . . . I saw myself writing a book about waking up and having it published. This was not a thought, but a full-fledged awareness of a natural development.

Thank you for the reminder of Gandhi's love of God—God as a bullet—I was very impacted when you told it in Mill Valley. It felt as if it penetrated a deep place, tucking it away as I realize the wonder of it, in the very moment of shock, being able to take in reality with grace and equanimity. What a fountain of grace to be aware of.

I am deeply grateful for your guidance; so helpful to have your pointers and hear about Anne's experience so maybe I don't need to freak out either, and I love you dearly.

Beth

JULY 19TH, 2013

Hi Beth.

It's wonderful to read what's going on. I wonder how it is for you now (you don't "need" to say; this is just a way of saying my heart goes toward you, whatever is happening).

You may feel less inclined, as time goes on, to share what's going on. Just saying it can be a mixed experience (for others and for you). But you will see whatever happens. I certainly understand the irresistible force of wanting to share it. How could you not? So long as you don't have expectations of any particular kind of response (or see the expectations, if some are there) whatever happens is just what happens.

Jan

JULY 21ST, 2013

Dear Jan,

I had a very unusual experience the other night. I was awakened out of a very deep sleep by what felt like an intense current of electricity coursing throughout my entire body. In a foggy state of awareness I realized I was in the midst of something brand new, never having had anything remotely similar happen, and so much not of "my" making. It was a strong jolt followed by a steady current. By the time I was able to get more conscious it had passed and I was left with the after-effects of tremendous heat. I had been in such a deep sleep that it seemed to take a long time to come to enough senses to register what I was feeling in my body, what might have happened, and how big and real it was. I wondered if it could be a stroke and if it was, was there something I needed to be doing about it. Thank goodness for Google! I began to search by typing in electric current in the body. Instead of leading me towards a stroke it brought me to a Kundalini awakening, which some part of me had already registered.

When I got back into bed I felt like I was having hot flash after hot flash, my entire body heating as it had when we were together in Mill Valley, after the fire cleansing the gut. And then I became aware of energy traveling up and down my spine.

I went back to sleep and that was that, at least for now.

I feel little inclination to say what is going on with me—the awakening appears to be becoming more absorbed. I still want to shout from the mountaintop and am almost always a hairbreadth away from full body laughing, but I am guessing this too will mature.

It is helpful to stay conscious that thoughts are coming from some other planet. I have moved from a worried keeping them at arm's length, worrying that they are poison I cannot afford to swallow, to letting them in so I can register them long enough to listen and then be able to cut them off at the root. The last few months of watching the true folly of my thoughts has been very helpful in not giving them the time of day now. Not to say they are not trying very, very hard to get my attention and convince me that they are reliable and true, but how quickly the moment passes!

Well, I could go on and on but I won't. I am beside myself with gratitude; I think about wanting a spiritual teacher and you showing up. I think about what it means to have you in my life and I know joy. It is mysterious and wondrous and I do not take any of it for granted.

Lots and lots of love Jan,

Beth

JULY 23RD, 2013

Good morning, dear heart.

Someone just cancelled a phone appointment for this time, so I'm happily able to respond to you just as I've read your message. It's a cool, dark, rainy morning here. Raining softly. This kind of rain always reminds me of a line in Shakespeare, "How the quality of mercy is not strained; it droppeth as the gentle rain from heaven..."

Reading about the current reminds me of some of Krishnamurti's descriptions of what he called the process (in his *Notebook*, which I think you read/have).

And just now I'm recalling how Franklin Merrell-Wolff refers to being "in the current" (which felt like it put words to my experience early on). He isn't talking about a physical sensation, more the bigger awareness (vs. the ordinary). I don't know whether you ever read his *Pathways Through to Space*, but if you didn't it might speak to you. Kind of stodgy old language, but even so, it's worth it.

My sense of the thoughts coming and all of that—and I think Adya may say some valuable things in *The End of Your World* (which might mean a whole new thing to you now; did you read it before?) Is that as it (the familiar structure) all unwinds, bits of it "visit," come to the surface on their way out (if not this time, the next), as a way of putting it in the face, making vivid just how the suffering has worked. Who knows? This too is just a story, this way of accounting for what's going on. But it all felt very benign to me, and I let it be . . . even as I had no idea what was going on (I mean, that awakening had happened). It's all just a phenomenon.

I'm not, by the way, encouraging you to read, if you aren't moved to. Just noticing my mention of several books. Only if you're moved in that direction.

I don't know if I already told you this. A couple of summers ago I invited some local-ish people to get together on my porch. Each had shared with me, over time, the experience of awakening; several were wide-awake, several sort of at the edges of it. But all had experienced significant shifts, bringing about noticeable changes in their ways of relating with people, etc. I had so loved being with each of them, savoring that dear company (which is why they sought me out, wanting it themselves, wanting to be with someone who got it). So I thought—how lovely it would be for them to have one another's company. I dreamed of it for a long time and finally actually brought it about. It was delicious, in so many ways. Just seeing how a bunch of "strangers" (to one another) encountered one another. None of the usual social structures. Utter comfort, spontaneity, the refreshing absence of self-consciousness. It was extraordinary. I just sat quietly and watched. As people began sharing, there were commonalities and also differences. But one of the things that people had very much in common was reporting that after an initial period of bursting to share this with their loved ones, they grew quiet about it, realizing they simply would not be understood. Or someone would think they understood but would not, or someone would understand but doubt the authenticity of what was reported, or be jealous, or be afraid the relationship would suffer, etc., etc. And then there is the gradual realization that (as you have already experienced) you can "share" this wordlessly and wonderfully, without any story ever being told. K. talks about this in a dialogue he had with David Bohm (physicist), something about how the ground of being is wherever you go, and it has its own way. How its "effect" is so big, so unknowable, and not needing to be directed by us. That is, even if you decide to never say another word, it will work its own magic.

This is reminding me of another story, and I do hope I'm not repeating myself, but so what (eh?) The first person I encountered to whom this had happened (some years before we met) said something very helpful to me, via *A Course in Miracles* (which was her "route" there). It was, by the way, an enormous blessing to encounter her (she heard about me—the first other person she knew of—and contacted me). I told her I was aching to be of help to others, and wanting to know what I might do (this was before my first book happened). She was so calm, so wise. She pointed me to a passage in *ACIM* that says, simply, "You need do nothing." I felt my whole body relax. I knew the truth of it, that the "what to do" would come in its own way, without my having to figure it out or direct it. And so it did, and does.

Oh Beth. My heart is full of joy, thinking of you, loving you so.
Jan

JULY 30TH, 2013

Dearest Jan,

Hello and greetings. Thank you for your email; your guidance and reflections help a lot. Perhaps more than you know and perhaps you do know.

Where to even step into the stream? You are with me always—as Life flows throughout.

The flow feels like silk passing through my fingers, moving moment to moment to moment.

And yet, everything is simple, practical, and every day.

And at times the silk snags on some sharp object. And moves on.

I am still reading *Krishnamurti's Notebook* and began a book of Maharishi's teachings.

I am not aware of any direct traces of the experience with the jolt of Kundalini electricity. I know that Krishnamurti lived with the physical discomfort most of the time and Irina Tweedie suffered mightily from it for five years. This might be a story but I do wonder if it is related to "cleansing" because what I seemed to "know" within and right after the jolt was a sense of a finishing touch—like a clearing of a—no, the, channel. Hard to really know though. I remember you saying many times that your knowing matured and developed over time, and what seemed apparent at the time was not so much later on.

I have been in so many traffic jams in the last couple of weeks. The Bay Bridge was closed unexpectedly (they found some suspicious package midway), and I was trying to get home. That time and today when traffic was backed up for miles I had the instinct to find another route and did so without effort. The other times I inched along until traffic opened up. I was aware each time of how fluid life was, passing along no matter what. And I had the sense of gliding. In fact, when traffic moves along I am gliding at the same time very present to the other cars, the road, and the signs.

I feel profoundly quiet.

The time with patients has been glorious since the shift. It is as if I have known each and every person for a long, long time (in some cases this is physically true) and am just now waking to the fact of how much I love them. They walk into my office and I feel this love in a quiet and steady way, and what I cannot get over is how different our time together is. The closest way I can describe it is by saying everything is so much more real. It is as if I am not sidetracked by the various ways they have of distorting. I have been a deep listener for a long time but I hear and take them in in an even more full and dimensional way. Even as I write this I am aware of not being able to capture what it is like—perhaps you know what I mean—from how you are with the people you work with. In fact, something about being with you and the others in Mill Valley settled into my pores; a way of being and presence that is alive every moment, especially and including when people are in the midst of knowing themselves more and more.

The mind gave me quite a tussle over the past weekend. After spending some time with a friend I found myself in a tizzy. As tumultuous as it was I was able to stay the course with sufficient equanimity. I questioned the reality of awareness and felt the pull of fear. I was reminded, once again, of Jesus' time in the desert— being besieged by the demons of the ego—the more light that was shining in, the more ego got scared and pulled out the stops. I can tell you I have a strong sense of something more, something left, needing to die. I remembered that you had mentioned not having to be a "regular" person, giving time to the shift, and I became aware of what that meant in the flesh, meaning this regular person was screaming to stay viable.

I didn't sleep one of the nights of the weekend, crazily and vigorously pushing the river, to let go, and, at the same time, aware and watching it all. Oddly, when I awoke in the morning after finally falling asleep, I felt the deep happiness and quiet that appears to be a steady stream in the background. It was so lovely. And being troubled by these thoughts is also different. It is as if the trouble and the thoughts are further away, not as large or noisy, and even though the ego is insistent on its truth, its voice holds less and less weight.

I read a striking example in Ramana's book: pictures of a fire burning everything are projected onto a screen or pictures of a major flood, destroying everything are projected on a screen. The screen is not burned or flooded; in fact it is untouched by the pictures streaming across its face. Isn't that a grand image for the unchanging and untouched vastness?

Well, dearest Jan; I didn't know what I would say to you when I sat down at my computer. I just know I want to be with you. So here we are.

Sending you lots of love and gratitude,
Beth

AUGUST 1ST, 2013

Hello, dear heart.

At last I have been able to give myself to this writing. I appreciate that you make the effort (knowing it will never be a perfect rendering, but doing it anyhow). It's lovely to be immersed in what it's been like for you these recent days.

This that you said—"Where to even step into the stream"—I experience it every time I sit with people, as I did last Sunday. I am so full, I hardly know what to start with (speaking, I mean). It's almost like I sit there with the sensation of a record turning, and the needle could set itself down anywhere at all. The silence went on for so long, the other night (us looking at one another, everybody waiting), that I finally said, "don't worry," and they laughed.

The screen image is apt. It's familiar to me from a video of a talk by Papaji. I saw it not too long after awakening. It was an amazing articulation of what I was experiencing.

Love, forever and always,
Jan

AUGUST 3RD, 2013

Experience in the grocery store:

I am standing at the produce section, having just pulled a plastic bag from above my head and looking at the cabbages, trying to see which one to pick up. I have a full body sensation of reaching back up for the plastic bags and become very disoriented because my arm is not moving upwards—all in a split second—I look immediately to my right and there is a woman pulling off a bag.

I feel dizzy.

It was a second of complete and total immersion and I couldn't distinguish her from me or vice versa.

* * *

Realization in the tub:

The love and openness I am is not personal.

The truth of this got my attention, in such sharp contrast to my previous assumption of what love is and what it feels like. Love is not controlling, has no agenda and moves/responds fully from what is actually happening.

Something is working inside towards being in the world and being with other people. After January I felt deeply called to be alone. After the retreat I have felt pulled to be with people/friends but the experiences have resulted in constriction.

* * *

"And turbulence is also observed!
One who is impacted upon is thinning away."

Mooji

AUGUST 4TH, 2013

Dearest Jan,

Again, where to even begin? I was awakened around midnight last night and began a deepening that revealed the nature of pure formless consciousness, realizing all that I am is that. And being that. Followed by a profound gentle awareness that there is no death, only a dissolving into the natural state. It appears that this took four hours because it was four in the morning when "I" came back, but it could have been one minute for all I knew.

In coming back into the body I had a moment of concern that there was more letting go, and then became aware that there was a skip in momentum upon coming back into the body—not so pleasant at first but no big deal after all. For one quick moment there was some disruption; wanting to stay there, feeling the letting go wasn't complete and then awareness that it was a resistance to coming back into the body.

This deepened and profound realization began today with being cranky. I had had three visits with friends that left me jangled.

I was out of sorts all day yesterday. I sat in the woods, I began Merrill-Wolff's book, I watched several snippets of Mooji, and lived with not knowing what was out of sorts.

In Merrill-Wolff's book I read how he searched for ultimate reality through the science he knew and by questioning the logic of his thinking. I thought, *hmm—using his mind and intelligence, not denying it.*

Mooji told a wonderful joke about God telling a seeker to let go, and the seeker believing he would die if he let go of the branch of the tree on a mountaintop asked for a second opinion. He also talked about the process of meeting the mind's artillery with strong artillery as well and watching the terror recede as "you" have more victories over the ego's insistence on steering.

Well, the midnight journey began with all the strong and unpleasant feelings that had been stirred up with the three visits with friends. I entered a state of terrible confusion and fear and countered it with an admonishment to let go. Something wise showed up showing Merrill-Wolff's intelligent process, softening my process and allowing the genuine inquiry. What is threatened, what is believed, etc. I was reminded of the invitation to see, really see with an open heart, the portal in so to speak. And rather than have an abstract understanding or mental concept, the process became real, very real (revealing the discomfort and upset's projections); and then opened into the profound vastness revealing "me" as pure formlessness, as was everything, everything. Every tree, building, gnat, and person. Alive, dynamic, and yet empty. Moving and formless.

The image of the seeker hanging from a branch high up on the side of a mountain showed up. From here, there was no falling to the ground splat. Letting go of the branch allowed a soft and easy dissolving into the formless, being absorbed in from whence "I" came. Water to water, ether-to-ether, God-to-God, and formless to formless.

Coming back into the body felt strange and familiar and I went back to sleep.

And now to close. There is no ending here so how about if I close for now . . .

With so much love and gratitude,
Beth

AUGUST 5TH, 2013

Beth,

Wow, laughing here, amazed at the process, and the language. This is glorious, looking from afar . . .

Funny, I was just yesterday writing to T. about Merrill-Wolff and "getting there" via the mind. Once a person is clear about the difference between the egoic use of the mind and the "clean" use of the mind, that blob in the head can be a door-opener.

Jan

AUGUST 6TH, 2013

I am aware of being all that is—all is consciousness—aware that what is revealed is a version of something too immense and un-knowable to be anything else but an approximation. A thin layer, a representation that shows the truth to the degree it is possible to be. And even with that being true it is like catching lightning in a bottle.

I was up most of last night with a steady current of electricity cruising throughout the entire body—limbs, torso, back, heart, head, and crown. Moments of more intensity around the heart, and moments of more volume in the neck and head.

Not comfortable, not painful though. But surging with enough energy to disallow falling asleep.

I read Franklin Merrill-Wolff—*Pathways Through to Space,*

"It seems that the inward penetration does make some demand upon the body."

He also writes about consciousness rising within at times and being quieter at others.

I feel a strong need to stay quiet, not arouse consciousness, so the body might rest.

Lightning in a bottle. Absorbing increased consciousness into everyday body and life. Awareness is aware of that.

AUGUST 12TH, 2013

There are streams of intensity
Everything is intense . . .
beauty, joy, fear, emptiness
Everything is felt, directly

I am sitting on a bench at the Palace of Fine Arts. The weeping willow tree is stunningly alive and vibrating—so full!

The swans, gulls, and pigeons, squawking, begging for food, flying and gliding to a stop into the water. People speaking different languages are strolling, taking pictures, laughing. The fog is thick and the wind is chilly. I am seeing Grecian architecture, with pigeons crowded on the ledges above Grecian maids.

Something catches my eye, across the lagoon. Near the top of a ledge a healthy and fit young woman in a bright red leotard is moving, moving, as if in tune to music and poetry, striking ballet poses. So quiet, no sound whatsoever from where I am sitting and without warning I am overwhelmed with tears and emotions of beauty and love. It is so strikingly beautiful—I melt.

* * *

Franklin Merrill-Wolff: *Pathways Through to Space.*

Personality:
"This Space is too large. Where are the comforting bars of the cage? I would like to return to the world that I know so well. I would like to move, inconspicuous, in the domain where I know my way. Release me from the Fire."

Intellectual man:
"Be still, thou foolish one. Those pastures and encircling walls thou cravest are barren and small before this Largeness. Be not like the canary bird that refuses the offered freedom, but come on with Me."

Real Man:

"Be patient, child, thou shalt be guarded and shalt find again all thou dost love. For this small travail, thou, too, shalt drink of the Waters of Immortality, which I AM. The limits of thy strength will not be forgotten."

The Current:

"I find that the Current is consumed, at least apparently so, in the expression of thought. I feel It less after casting It into form. It seems to have gone forth in a kind of new birth. Yet I am happy this should be so. The Fount is exhaust less, and there remains—enough."

And amen to that—may this one also take solace from that reminder.

It is reassuring to read others write about the immensity of the changes needed in the body to withstand and vibrate with the profound energies and intensities. It helps me understand, have a context for what feels like being re-arranged. And what it means to embody love and consciousness in a real and abiding way.

AUGUST 14TH, 2013

Dear Jan,

Hello again. I woke up this morning having dreamt about you, for the second or third time actually, and each time you are in a different form, no surprise. I realize though that I would like to talk to you about fear. Just in case I am either missing something or on the wrong track and not helping matters.

Everything, I mean everything, is intensified. I cry at beauty and love—I pick up subtle cues of what others are feeling and feel it in the body, not even sure who is feeling. When I am giddy it is full steam ahead, when I am happy it is bigger than the body, and so on and so on.

My sleep is very disturbed. I had been sleeping well after our retreat but the deepening and surges of energy and "current" typically happen in the middle of the night. Added to this: I have a bone spur (source of pain) and had the nail removed for the time being in preparation for surgery. I twisted the other ankle walking in the Presidio and it swelled up pretty badly, and yesterday I sat in the dentist's chair for over four hours.

All of this to say that I am experiencing fear from the adrenals being triggered. I can actually feel the cortisol in the body.

I can ease into the fear at times and ride the wave, and even at times dip into the peace below and around. Last night, after a long bout of anxiety in the dentist's chair, I settled gently and deeply into letting go.

But many times I am afraid of the fear. I have discovered a treatment of brain-feedback/training that helps people with PTSD, insomnia, anxiety, etc. and I am going for a consultation this Friday. The person who recommended it to me says he now sleeps easily and consistently after two years of Kundalini interruptions so it is at least worth checking out. That being said, though, what I wonder is when to pay attention to what might be going on in the relative state and know it needs proper care, and when to surrender even that. When to take care of what is frightened and when to let it go? From where I sit it makes sense to take care of the body as is possible and stay present to each awakened moment, giving over whenever called for.

What does it look like from there?

Love,

Beth

AUGUST 15TH, 2013

Beth,

It's great that you are looking so carefully (everywhere, it seems, but even here too).

One of the blessings of greater clarity (and less attachment) is that it has become possible to distinguish between actions-taken-out-of-fear and "legitimate" actions taken to minimize difficulty (in the outward sense of that—not to minimize angst but to make life simpler, more able to flow easily, including in a bodily sense). You are looking at a bodied response that is in bed with fear, so I can imagine this being tricky, this distinction.

Let go of the tendency to second-guess yourself. There is a higher something at work here. When you go to the higher knowing, you know what to do. There is no fear there, only clarity.

When the physical response is triggered, sit with the sensation, in complete surrender, and if there is a story coming up, or image, or resistance, or whatever, just see that as phenomenon. See it for what it is. When you are worrying about the adrenals, see the story/image that is the juice behind the worry.

It's good you see at times you are afraid of the fear. Surrender to that too. Don't try to manage anything.

That last thing you said sounds right on to me—"take care of the body as is possible and stay present to each awakened moment, giving over whenever called for." Taking care of the body is in no way "contrary," of course, to staying present to the moment. Sometimes attention to the body is the "door."

About this: "Pay attention to what might be going on in the relative state." At some point you may see that the idea of the relative state doesn't occur to you so much. That dual perception can have a feeling of one mode being more authentic than the other, or less egoic, or something like that. You might find it helpful to look at experience/perception/awareness as degrees of being "zoomed out" or in. The more zoomed in you are, the more aware of the physical you are (and all that goes with that—the particular, the separate, the sensory, etc.). It all comes with "pretending" to be a person. The more zoomed out your awareness is, the more distant you may feel from pain, mental handling, etc.

Everything is relative to everything else (how's that for a useless pronouncement?) Just saying that depending on where you are, at the moment, along that scale, it's authentic, from that perspective. It's real, from where you're looking from and experiencing. You could get "way out there" and watch yourself going through all of this, but then, from that point of view, you wouldn't (couldn't) be doing anything to help yourself.

I hope this is helpful somehow.

Loving you . . .

Jan

Hello,

This has been so helpful—sitting with the sensation, recognizing and watching the juice behind the fear, and having it be clearer is making a big difference. I am easily sitting with what is and there is something about the zooming in and out that settles something inside and is allowing this movement (of going back and forth) to go more smoothly.

After this email conversation between us I had a dream that awoke me:

I was in a room with other people and a woman came up to me and (knowing I would have no recollection whatsoever) told me that she had made love to me. I am made aware that this is pointing to a completely unknown time/experience that from this perspective looks completely dark and black (no content, story, at all). She leans into me and whispers into my ear that this is the body memory and I am then gratefully aware that I now know something I need to know. In the dream I feel a deep, deep sadness and the woman leaves the room. Another woman, who appears to be facilitating whatever activity is going on, looks at me and nods that she is aware of what has transpired, meaning it has not gone unrecognized or acknowledged.

That awakens me, and I am aware, now being awake, that this is all I need to know and that this awareness can help "me" be kind and gentle with the body. Something is eased even further into letting go.

Then this morning I met with the man who does the brain training. There were several books in his room about awakening, including one he and his wife wrote, having interviewed many awakened people, including Adya. We had an hour conversation and what struck me the very most is: "When the brain sees itself it moves into complete harmony." Is that not gorgeous! It brought me to tears. The neuro-feedback is an intensive process that appears gentle and effective (for one thing in easing insomnia) and everything in me is saying yes to it.

I left his office feeling great gratitude; it does appear that no matter what shows up there are openings for movement. My God!

So Jan, a continuous thank you along with amazement,
Beth

* * *

This go around solitude is not nourishing as it was in the winter and spring. I want company these days—and yet . . . only if it is real connecting—not a distraction or a diversion—on either of our parts.

And . . . not a stone is unturned. Everything, everything is being burned, looked at, felt, seen, and most times dissolved.

Some more from Franklin Merrell-Wolff's *Pathway Through to Space*:

"There are subtle violences and inquiries injuries that are very difficult to describe, since their symptoms are of quite different quality from the familiar sensations of the gross body. There is a place of fine-edged balance in the mind that once destroyed the whole structure crashes . . ."

Such a helpful bigger picture—seeing the transition! No wonder about being vulnerable, disoriented, and discombobulated. I appreciate finding words to this experience . . . to this radical shift.

"The whole structure crashes" somehow touches a spot that rings more true than saying dying. Masks, costumes, pretending, roles, unconsciousness, history, and loneliness—the structures erected to form my personality are showing themselves. Many of them are simply evaporating into thin air. Others seem to be more entrenched. It seems to be a gradual crash . . .

Jan is coming back to California for a large retreat in August.

AUGUST 27TH, 2013

I am on retreat with Jan—a weekend in Novato—She has come out to California and is doing several satsangs in different cities and then a weekend for those folks who are interested and ready for looking deeper. There is a core group of women who have hosted Jan before (a few years ago) and they are having a small gathering for a couple of hours before the weekend retreat begins. Jan has invited me to join this smaller group gathering and I am also going to the retreat.

I haven't seen Jan, in person, since our time together in Mill Valley and I am giddy with the prospect of seeing her. I drive up to Sebastopol for her first satsang and feel a schoolgirl flush when I see her get out of the car.

I go to each of her satsangs and soak in the love. I feel as if I am floating through space. It is beyond measure to have such access (to her, to me, to love, to joy) . . . like a shy teenager being invited to the dance . . . and even more to the point, being able to relish it all, not missing what it is like to be there, at the dance, in real time.

The retreat is full. I know many of the people who are there. I am staying at my cousin's house as she lives nearby. I attend the retreat during the day and visit with my cousin and her husband a bit in the evenings. Their home is in the woods and I enjoy sitting out on the deck.

On the third evening of the retreat:

I am in bed not sleeping. I realize I am not sleepy.

The current is sweet and present, filling the entire body.

I am more able to be at ease with not sleeping.

And hang out with the physical sensations.

I fall asleep and am aware of presence like a sweet perfume.

I am aware of not thinking at all and the sweet peace of that.

I have a dream:

I need to find a clean copy of my dissertation on the computer. The copies I already have are filled with corrections like a work in progress. I get an accurate copy, but it looks different than I remember it. It is more rich, detailed, and full of color.

As soon as I get it the man sitting next to me abruptly sits up when he sees that the entire computer is crashing. There is another man behind me who is a computer expert and he looks on in amusement. As if to indicate it will crash no matter what. Don't bother with the fuss.

The man next to me is getting panicked and tells me the computer is crashing from an internal source of water.

A frenzied man runs in the room disbelieving. A bit mad.

Someone says "accept what is."

Franklin Merrill-Wolff: "The whole system is crashing!" From an internal source of water!

* * *

I float through the retreat—I am carried by, immersed in pure presence and love—floating/empty—so gloriously empty. I watch and listen as Jan speaks and people in the room reach out to her. I register everything—in a neutral and unresisting fluidity. It is like watching vapor or clouds—recognizable and interesting, but always ultimately evaporating. Actually it is being vapor, being clouds. That is what it is like to breath in and out of every moment, the now. What used to bring an apparent substance (thinking and identification with roles, history, and memory) is not operating. Instead, the emptiness reflects everything happening now.

There is a man in the audience who cries loudly, off and on, as Jan speaks. There is so much space for this to happen, even though some in the audience are uncomfortable. At one point, as Jan is speaking (and the man is almost wailing) she excuses herself and goes over to him to give him a hug. He tells of being violently raped when he was a child. There is so much silence in the room, as if everyone is hugging him, not just Jan.

Throughout the weekend I feel utter peacefulness. It is a total freedom of being with what is, everything that is—every person in the room, every molecule of life as it is in this room, in this courtyard, the anguish in the young man's tears, the clouds drifting by—everything is so still and movingly alive.

My God, how totally cool—I feel as if I have been given the keys to heaven.

SEPTEMBER 2ND, 2013

Dear Jan,

I began writing to you with all this being true:

I miss being with you in person.

I would love to curl up in comfortable chairs on your porch and chat.

What I can't get over is how, ultimately, it was so very gentle. Both in Mill Valley and the week in Northern California, being with you eased whatever to fully shift into place/"home." And even as thoughts are observed, feelings felt, patterns of relationships/ friendships tugged at, (knowing there is seventy years of being "the other way" being drained right out of me), there is no separation—you had wisely suggested to me after our time in Mill Valley that even what doesn't feel good is God. Wow, you can say that again!

I read today in Merrell-Wolff: "Man is no longer incarnated there, in the usual sense, and sooner or later dissolution will finally liquidate the apparent embodiment. This temporary continuation is like the continued revolving of the flywheel of an engine from which the power has been shut off. The engine is stopped in the essential sense, and will become fully stopped shortly."

The other thing Merrell-Wolff is helping with is confirmation of the demand of the body. I am needing to pay a great deal of attention to my body—everything from the chronic pain left over from surgery that got flared by sitting too long on hard chairs, to the extra energy, heat, and electrical currents interfering with sleep, and especially the demands on the body coming from the major transformative changes going on inside. I realize as I write this that there is no fear any longer with this.

Well, included in all this—there are a few friends who are reaching out unhappy with things not being the same between us. I need some help with one in particular. Many months ago he called me and said he was worried about me, and so I said perhaps it was time to at least give him a gist of what changes were going on in me. We met and I told him how happily blissful I was—being fully immersed in this process. We talked for a couple of hours, with him continuing to say he was worried about me.

He went away for summer vacation and called me when he returned hoping we could get together again. I could tell from his message something was up.

We had the same conversation. He says, you are distant—yes, I say, that is true. He says I feel as if I have lost a friend and I say yes, things are radically different inside me and everything that has been familiar is melting away. He asks what my other friends and sons are saying to me and about me. He says he cannot even ask me what is going on since I seem so distant. I tell him a bit more about the internal experience (knowing full well we are speaking totally different languages and trying to communicate truthfully and with awareness). I can actually feel his pain and struggle to get things back to where they were and I am aware of not wanting to or being able to do that. I tell him I am aware of this likely being difficult for him and want him to know I realize that.

He again says he is worried about me.

This conversation troubled me. I went through many emotions and even some confusion. Sitting with it, it became clear that something was wanting to be said, and I sat with that for a couple of days—I told him that the biggest change in me is that the divine and surrender are everything to me. It had appeared to me over time that he was not keen on that, and in fact, turned off. We attempted to talk this through and I realized he was hearing it in terms of whose fault it was that we were in conflict. I said I was not seeing any fault here, not in him and not in me, but acknowledging there is a block between us that keeps us from being close.

I give you all these details for help in background and context—I am left with a whirling of a drama that, as it appears, holds no real interest to me. And yet, it is taking up a great deal of energy and thought, and I have to wonder if there is some attachment in here for me. I feel his pain and I feel his panic around all this loss.

You know, I am aware that relationships have been an issue throughout the awakening process—I do live in the world and have many ties—I would love to walk this sensitively and tenderly—several of my friends were in the retreat with us. I had a fantasy that now (after being with you) they would understand my preference for silence, solitude, and my lack of interest in being social simply for social-sake. But it appears it cannot go like that.

I think I will stop here even though, as always, I could go on and on—oh, one more quick thing. I met up with the man who had been violated in his youth after everyone else had left the retreat. I found myself walking up to him, asking if we could talk, telling him that I shared his history, and wanted him to know that it was gone, completely gone. We spoke for quite a while and I gave him my card in case he would like a referral from me. You know, Jan, somehow this all seems a bit related. I was very taken by the different ending you had for the elevator visualization. You said, "you hear people crying." My body leaned forward spontaneously.

Love is indiscriminate, not attached or personal.

Well, I really am going to stop. Thank you dearest one.

Lots and lots of love,

Beth

SEPTEMBER 4TH, 2013

It would be lovely for us to sit on my porch one fine day.

What you wondered about whether there is attachment in this relationship stuff—not necessarily; but the deeper point is that the subtle radar of being alert to possible signs of unconsciousness should be allowed to unwind. Anything that needs to be seen will be seen and dealt with. You don't need any filters of understanding/labeling/etc. They only get in the way, obscuring what needs to happen, to be seen.

Before I lose track of this, just to say—I'm glad you encountered that man with the similar history, glad for him.

If I ever write another book, if there is anything that could sufficiently compel me, it would be on what happens to relationships.

That all of it stirs you up and has you wondering about attachment is natural, not surprising. Our only way of being with someone that you've known a long time is to sort of slip into the persona that related to the person all these years. Their image of you has become, in a way, your image of yourself. It has always been that way—we become, with that person, who they think we are—but now when that familiar pattern occurs, it's uncomfortable to you because you no longer believe that's who you are. Yet your friends expect and need you to be that person. So in a way, automatically, you accommodate. There's no way to "go there" without the remnants of egoic stickiness being felt . . . including things like attachment, fear, etc. Also, what's going on is love. Because you love this person, you do feel their pain, concern, etc. That can be reminiscent of attachment, because in the past your love for them was egoic in nature. The love is still there, but the garbage that used to be woven into love is gone or fading away. They cannot experience the form your love is now taking (impersonal, unconditional). You feel their projections onto you. It's unavoidable.

I hope something here sheds light.

Love,

Jan

* * *

"It is said that Hafiz was ground to dust by his Master over a forty-year period and thus became nothing

I am a hole in
a flute

that the Christ's breath
moves
through

listen to that music"

HAFIZ
Love Poems from God

OCTOBER 12TH, 2013

Dear Jan,

All I can say is wow! I am so moved that it is real and steady—life is easy, simple, and honestly, being reality rocks! You and others have sounded the siren of it being possible to be happy just because; feeling endless depths of joy and being the openness of every single moment, without protest or opinion. To discover the truth of this sends me into ecstasy.

There is a new bay bridge in town and for many, many months I drove across the old one watching the new one be built an arm's throw away. Now the new one is finished and it is much wider and expansive, it appears to skim the waters below (meaning the view is one of no barrier), it is graceful and beautiful, and driving across I watch as the old one is dismantled. The workhorse, narrow and worn is now observable from a different perspective.

And so it is . . . Merrell-Wolff's language comes to mind: "Awakened Consciousness and Subjective-Objective Consciousness."

I did the neuro-feedback process I had mentioned to you—to help with insomnia. It appears to have helped. It was a five day process which ended a little over a week ago and I have slept easily more nights than not. I am falling asleep gently and even when waking in the middle of the night falling back to sleep—all without any medication. Not only am I very grateful for this help I am struck by how natural it feels; like, of course. Well, not only does it seem to have shifted a deep sleep pattern it also is showing up in other ways as well. I have always run cold and now I am frequently warm, when I would have been cold; in fact, at times too warm which has been unheard of. But even more amazing is that the background/undercurrent anxiety I have lived with most of my remembered life is draining away, slowly and undeniably. Everything is slower now. Without the motor of anxiety most moments are close (right there) and open; so open I can taste it. Oddly, these slow moments appear to be endless, how can such a quick moment be so open-ended.

And when the moments of anxiety habitually show up, they too are in slow motion and don't seem to have much if any weight; there's so much less to hook onto that I can even sense or imagine it being completely out of the picture. And what I can't get over is how natural all this is happening. "I" am not doing anything.

I can't help thinking about you and when fear falls away.

While sitting in the chair for the neuro-feedback sometimes I needed to have my eyes closed and other times open and reading. The practitioner's shelves were full of awakened teacher's books. I had forgotten that you had suggested David Carse to me when we were together last winter so I encountered him for the first time last week—oh, my goodness. What a light and what exquisite clarity (and funny, so funny). I took away what it was like for him after, and the respect for the amount of time the shift requires in order to "rearrange" the body and mind to the full bore of consciousness and energy. Something in me relaxed.

I loved, I think obviously, his trials with other people in his life. He wrote about people thinking he had lost his mind, but at least he was a happy idiot! If I remember what I read correctly, he came to the place of not talking about his state and carried on with his life as a carpenter in a quiet way.

Which brings me to relationships. I cannot tell you how helpful you were in your previous email about the issue of being with friends and family. I have been digesting what you said and watching as things unfold in front of my eyes.

I have us as a model—it appears to me that, amongst other factors, your unconditional and unceasing love brought me home. I know this love in my bones and it carries/surrounds everything like the divinity it is. I know this inside and, as funny as it sounds, being big/spacious enough to "take care of others," especially without them knowing the full extent of it, feels familiar to me in the way of knowing something before knowing it. When I first read it, and for days after, I felt a gush of warmth of recognition throughout my body. It literally thrilled me.

Anyway, being with others recently has given lots of opportunity to notice things like the desire in me to be understood, not to be disliked, or making anyone upset or angry. And again, the amazement of this showing up and dissipating just as quickly. "I" don't have to do anything with it, even when I, at times, tripped on myself by asking for understanding or sympathy. Like when I whined to my family that I was in physical pain and went on a bit looking for some sort of attention or recognition; and almost immediately seeing what was going on and it disappearing, really, really disappearing without a trace (as you often say, as gone as the big bang). This also brings David Carse to mind—he called his personality "that david thing" after his awakening and said he watched it blowing in the wind like sheets on a clothesline. Love it.

For me, it feels like a convert who looks back and cannot believe how it used to be. I can now see the pervasive language of living in the illusion of separation—from what is good and what is bad, to each and every thing that shouldn't be this way, to surely you still have some unhappiness ("pain body" in Eckhart's words), to the attempt to control other people's behavior. The gap between these worlds, on one hand, appears a fraction apart and on the other hand, unbridgeable. This probably also speaks to how I feel being with the friends with whom I have a long history. Everything is so familiar and everything is so strange. And even though I am not stirred very much, when with them these days I fully prefer solitude.

And a few things I want to tell you:

I am still getting a lot out of Merrell-Wolffs's book. Do you remember his metaphor of the caterpillar and butterfly—representing relative or subjective/objective consciousness and transcendent consciousness? Fabulous imagery.

I am going to Mt. Arunachala in January for four weeks of silence, meditation, walking around the mountain, and meeting with local awakened souls. Yukio Ramana leads a pilgrimage and has for over fifteen years. I remember sitting with you on the very first day of our visit in the winter and saying I am dying to climb a mountain and throw my arms into the air with ecstasy and joy and freedom.

With so much love,

Beth

OCTOBER 14TH, 2013

Such a blessing to read this, Beth.

I feel as if I'm getting to watch myself all over again (even as I realize we aren't "the same," but you know, there is so much that's familiar).

I'm happy you have had good results from the neuro-feedback. And how delicious that you'll have that time with the mountain. Wow.

You make me want to read Merrell-Wolff again.

I was at a retreat in Raleigh last weekend. I was one of maybe six teachers. I went last year as well. What a pleasure to be in that company, to see and hear how "it" manifests in various ways, how it gets expressed in teachings, in language. It's fun to attend something— to not always be on. Each teacher is up in front for about ninety minutes, and the rest of the weekend we're just "in the audience," meeting informally with attendees, eating wonderful food, walking around the woods. It's an annual event sponsored by a self-inquiry group in Raleigh. Now I'm getting ready for another retreat (pretty close by) next weekend. After that, things slow down a bit.

I love you dearly,

Jan

OCTOBER 20TH, 2013

Welcome home from your latest retreat Jan.

I enjoyed reading about your time in Raleigh, not only for its lusciousness in itself but also because it brought to mind how I felt about being with you both in Mill Valley and Northern California. Getting to be there, listen in every regard possible (without being on), and being in the audience. The retreat in Raleigh sounds magnificent, lucky people who attend.

I am sitting at home (since Wednesday) recovering from foot surgery and how's this for amazing—in the moments of intense pain there is no fear. You know for the longest time, I mean the longest time, I have had a sense that every pain I felt was exaggerated by fear. I could even say that out loud but could not let go enough to try it out. Not that I didn't try. And here it is and it is true. There were a couple of nights of pain that were really intense and lo and behold being it, fully not resisting it, didn't particularly diminish the felt sense of it, but it was oddly pure (not tinged with fear). I wasn't trying to do anything; meaning it showed up naturally and there is something about it not being pleasant or having felt "good" that made an impression on me. How about that? I thought, and remembered Gandhi and "Ram." Not that the pain from a surgical procedure, an elected one at that, is in the camp of being shot by someone who wants you dead. But from the standpoint of whatever is, is and in it's being so, comes and goes. I deeply knew this would not last and that whatever else showed up would and could be lived.

I have not had any pain for the last day or so. I am feeling physically tired and can you believe this? I am able to fall asleep, even with my foot elevated on two pillows and being limited to staying on my back.

I had a delightful conversation with a woman the other day. She was on a month-long retreat, read your book, and had an awakening. Our conversation was right "there" leaving both of us grateful for the knowing and the company; she might be in contact with you in the near future. But the more immediate point is how deliciously satisfying it is to make these contacts.

I think I will go back to the couch and have a long restful evening before going back to work tomorrow.

Lots and lots and lots of love,

Beth

November 5th, 2013

Beth,

I can't believe so long has gone by since you wrote this. I was so glad to hear about the pain (sans fear). I imagine by now you're very much on the mend.

I have been letting myself just be a slug these recent days—well, except for what has absolutely needed doing. It's been lovely to slow down. No more traveling now till January.

When are you off to—is it India?

I think of having a phone conversation with you, welcoming hearing how things are with you, plus things I'd like to share with you, but also about the color of my car; yes, very mysterious. I just like the idea of connecting. Not a "session," though who knows what such a thing would even be like now?

Anyhow, depending on when you'll be gone, maybe we can work it out, if it has appeal for you. My preference would be to wait till after my fall writing workshops are done (the end being the week before Thanksgiving week).

Buckets of love,

Jan

NOVEMBER 7TH, 2013

Hello dear Jan,

It is almost one o'clock here in California and I am in my pajamas puttering around to my heart's content. My practice is bulging these days and I am still not fully mobile because of the foot surgery so I am very happy to have a whole day of quiet.

How's this for "and what is it like 'after?'" I reached into the cupboard to see if I had any lentils and an entire bag of black beluga lentils (I tell you what kind so you can envision how little each lentil is) upends and scatters across the counter and floor. And I went, "oh, what fun—would you look at that?" They made a pretty design and I enjoyed going about gathering as many as I could salvage and cleaning up the rest.

I would love to connect by phone and have a visit.

Tons of love to you,

Beth

NOVEMBER 8TH, 2013

Being a full human. I am feeling vulnerable with my toe not yet healed so when I am out in public it takes extra energy to stay clear of other people's steps.

I am watching as I feel sad, cranky, tired, and limited—it is hard when I feel physically unwell or tired.

There is an amazing difference in energy when I am rested. And at same time, I notice there is loads more energy in my system even when I am tired.

NOVEMBER 9TH, 2013

I am grateful to the poets who proceeded in these apparent turbulent waters and can eloquently express what is deeply known in the marrows of our beings. Thank you.

"Whoever You Are Holding Me Now in Hand"
by Walt Whitman:

"Whoever you are, holding me now in hand,
Without one thing, all will be useless,
I give you fair warning, before you attempt me further
I am not what you supposed, but far different.

Who is he that would become my follower?
Who would sign himself a candidate for my affections?

The way is suspicious—the results uncertain, perhaps
Destructive:
You would have to give up all else—I alone would
expect to be your God, sole and exclusive,
Your novitiate would even then be long and exhausting
The whole past theory of your life, and all conformity to
the lives around you, would have to be abandon'd;
Therefore release me now, before troubling yourself any
Further—Let go your hand from my shoulders,
Put me down, and depart on your way.

Or else, by stealth, in some wood, for trial,
Or back of a rock, in the open air,
(For in any roof'd room of a house I emerge not—
nor in company,
and in libraries I lie as one dumb, a gawk, or unborn,
or dead),
But just possibly with you on a high hill—
first watching lest any person, for miles
around approach unawares,
Or possibly with you sailing at sea, or on the beach of
the sea, or some quiet island,
Here to put your lips upon mine I permit you,
With the comrade's long-dwelling kiss, or the new
husband's kiss,
for I am the new husband, and I am the comrade.

160

Or, if you will, thrusting me beneath your clothing,
Where I may feel the throbs of your heart, or rest upon
your hip,
carry me when you go forth over land or sea;
for thus, merely touching you, is enough—is best,
and thus, touching you, would I silently sleep and
be carried eternally.

But these leaves conning, you con at peril,
For these leaves, and me, you will not understand,
They will elude you at first, and still more afterward—
I will certainly elude you,
Even while you should think you had unquestionably
caught me, behold!
Already you see I have escaped from you.

For it is not what I have put into it that I have
written this book,
Nor is it by reading it you will acquire it,
Nor do those know me best who admire me, and
vauntingly praise me,
Nor will the candidates for my love, (unless at most
a very few), prove victorious,
Nor will my poems do good only—they will do just
as much evil, perhaps more;
for all is useless without that which you may guess
at many times and not hit—that which I hinted at;
therefore release me, and depart on your way."

* * *

Spiritual Warfare by Jed Mckenna:

"*Waking up from the dreamstate is a very straightforward busi-*
ness. It doesn't take decades. It doesn't look like tranquility or like a
calm, peaceful mind. It doesn't look like saving others or saving the

world or even saving yourself. It doesn't look like a thriving mar-
ketplace where merit is determined by popular appeal or commer-
cial success. Waking up looks like a massive mental and emotional
breakdown because that's exactly what it is, the granddaddy of all
breakdowns. That's the only way it works. I know there are thou-
sands of books out there that say otherwise, and I can tell you they
were all written by Maya. Once you understand what Maya is,
once you see her for yourself, that becomes perfectly obvious. You'd
see it like you see the sky."

* * *

"Seizing my life in your hands,
you thrashed it clean on the
savage rocks of Eternal Mind.

How its colors bled, until they grew white!
You smile and sit back; I dry in your sun."

RUMI

I find it so fulfilling to read words that can at least approximate
what "cleaning out, thoroughly cleaning out" is like from the inside out! Thank you dear Rumi, thank you Walt Whitman, thank
you Jed McKenna from the bottom of my heart.

* * *

Jed Mckenna:

"I'm defining the dreamstate as the state in which a person sees
what's out there and doesn't see what is; eyes closed, imagining re-
ality instead of eyes open, observing it. With eyes closed, one is
forced to live in an imagined, constantly conjured faux-reality."

We humans are continually destroying the universe with a
thought—living inside a thought-made, imagined, constantly

conjured faux-reality. It is amazing to see this from the "other" side. It is still close enough at hand to be able to taste and watch the made-up world of my conditioned mind at the same time as seeing things as they really are.

* * *

November 10th, 2013

Hi Jan,

Well, I went about the day after we finished our being together and thoroughly enjoyed the ease and flow of moving from one thing to another. And I realized a couple of things in the process. There is such a strong pull to being with what I want and less and less willingness to have it be different.

For instance—an open-ended "schedule"—after we hung up I found myself walking to the nearby forest of trees, finding a path less familiar and sitting, sitting quietly amongst the logs and trees. Later when I went to the grocery store I noticed how much I enjoy meeting and having brief interactions with the sales people.

And then, realizing the obligation I felt to give P. a call and how I certainly could do that but what if I didn't and let it openly flow into . . . who knows what? What about giving over to life flowing through? Coming home and watching a bit of a documentary on the assassination of JFK and then, as I was so moved, making cranberry sauces, I felt freed up from the pressing assumption that I needed to call P. in a certain amount of time, etc. How amazing . . . the nitty gritty of what it means to recognize and give over to what's really in charge.

I love the work I do and yet I am feeling pinched by the constraint and lack of being able to naturally flow from whatever to whatever. In the "human" realm I would say to myself, "suck it up you have to be an adult here." And now?

David Hawkins in *Power vs. Force* writes:

"The skillfull are not obvious
They appear to be simple-minded

163

Those who know this know the patterns of the Absolute
To know the patterns is the Subtle Power
The Subtle Power moves all things and has no name."

I am so pulled to what appears to be simple-minded; moving as so moved. I bet this is what is moving inside me these days, finally bubbling up to the light of day, and what it might mean in the way I live in the external world.

Also realizing the subtle shifts of sand as I relate to you . . . only knew after that it seemed important to not look to you as teacher (given the strong pattern of dependency I have lived within) and instead allow the knowing to bubble from within. Hence, it appears now, some of my tongue-tied babbling while we were on the phone, and the subsequent clarity of some things.

It means a great deal to be able to travel this with you. Thank you, really!

I briefly glanced through David Hawkins' *Power vs. Force* and he has a fascinating distinction for the different levels of vibrations and energy for the awakened state, distinguishing amongst unconditional love (calibrated at 500) and inner joy (540). "[T]he hallmark of this state is compassion. People who have attained this level have a notable effect on others. They're capable of a prolonged, open visual gaze, which indicates a state of love and peace"—to peace (600) associated with . . . transcendence, self-realization, and God-consciousness. Of this he says, "It's extremely rare, attained by only one in ten million people. When this state is reached, the distinction between subject and object disappears, and there's no specific focal point of perception . . . Perception at the level of 600 and above is sometimes reported as occurring in slow motion, suspended in time and space—nothing is stationary, and all is alive and radiant. Although this world is the same as the one seen by others, it has become continuously flowing, evolving in an exquisitely coordinated evolutionary dance in which significance and source are overwhelming . . ." And then onto enlightenment (700-1,000). "At this level, there is no longer the experience of an individual personal self separate from others; rather, there is an identification of Self with Consciousness and Divinity. . ."

Fascinating, isn't it? On one hand, I wonder if it is really possible to delineate—really—knowing there are moments and glimpses of all that he describes, and on the other hand, I think about Jed McKenna's "further" which rings inside as true. Moments and glimpses can and will become a norm. That is true at least over here.

This, too, is what tickles me about being in the flow: Hawkins' work coming up in our conversation and now revisiting it and letting it simmer.

And lastly, I feel a sense of awe at being alive, whole, and divine in this human form and all it asks and gives.

The delightful tale of your car has lingered with me all day, with great warmth.

Lots and lots of love, Jan

Beth

* * *

Hello again Jan,

I am reading (and weeping) David Hawkins' awakening (in *Power vs. Force*) and feel his words deep in my solar plexus. I couldn't have articulated this and yet it speaks loudly of some deep knowing and a deeper recognition of what appears to be moving around inside.

"The ecstasy that accompanies this condition (Love of the Presence) isn't absolutely stable; keep in mind that there are also moments of great agony. The most intense moments occur when the state fluctuates and suddenly ceases for no apparent reason. These times bring on periods of intense despair, a fear that one has been forsaken by the Presence. These falls make the path arduous, and to surmount these reversals requires great will. It finally becomes obvious that one must transcend this level or constantly suffer excruciating descents from grace. The glory of ecstasy then has to be relinquished, as one enters upon the demanding task of transcending duality, until one is beyond all oppositions and their conflicting pulls. But while it's one thing to happily give up the iron restraints of the ego, it's quite another to abandon the golden

chains of ecstatic joy—it feels as if one is giving up God, and a new level of fear arises, never before anticipated; this is the final terror of absolute aloneness."

This is what I have been deeply intuiting!

In my own case, the fear of nonexistence was formidable, and I drew back from it repeatedly. When you asked us in Mill Valley what we are most afraid of, I knew without a shadow of a doubt it was annihilation—very different than death.

Somehow this context brings tears of relief and great gratitude. It has certainly appeared as if there is some death looming and yet whenever I looked nothing showed up. I have been very used to finding a story, feeling, belief, or something that needed to be let go, but this is different.

Whew, what a day . . . as the spirit continues to move and again, thank you so much for our time together this morning—so much fruit and open doors (to mix metaphors, oh well!)

Giant love,

Beth

* * *

Hawkins is pointing to something that captures my attention—likely the fluctuation of the state of being after awakening. I am keenly aware of the turbulence involved in embodying the presence and stillness that we are. Having it reflected, so clearly, helps the navigation process and I am very grateful.

I also have a sense he is pointing to something more I can only intuit, something beyond this observing awareness of awareness so to speak. The sense I have here is the same I had most of my life—there is something I recognize, remember, but do not have immediate access to at this moment.

NOVEMBER 12TH, 2013

Good morning, dear heart.

Thank you for all of this, for Hawkins and for your reflections.

I woke up to a white world, the first of the season. So lovely. And very cold. I'm giving a talk tonight. I wonder if anyone will venture out. According to the forecast, it's supposed to feel like it's zero tonight.

I'm often struck by a kind of innocence, or . . . don't know what to call it . . . that seems to have attended my process (and maybe still does). When I read or hear others describe their experience (fear, awareness of movement to a «new phase,» or recoiling from some kind of transition), I think—did I/do I have an equivalent experience? What I chalk it up to (historically, anyhow) is that I truly was innocent about what was happening. I hadn't read all the books, heard all the teachers, encountered others who had already gone through it. Is this why?

That said, I have often experienced great pleasure, especially early on, reading what others have said, and the pleasure has been of the nature of recognition, of the familiar. Most keenly this occurred reading Merrell-Wolff and Krishnamurti. Oh, and Tolle.

I may have mentioned on the phone, not sure, but I've been reading some old writing of my own, and I've been struck on several occasions by descriptions of things that were happening (years before awakening) that indicate now, in retrospect, a ground-preparation. Things of which I had no memory. When I remember the night fear left, I always think (and say) that I had no sense of readiness for such a thing, that it was quite out of the blue. And it was, it truly was; yet when I read this old stuff, I see a lot was going on (duh) before. I think it's just that I never imagined I was headed toward awakening, so I didn't pay attention in that way.

There was a moment in Novato that came back to me yesterday when you said something about your relationship with me. It was when we sat down together on the floor, in the hallway around the corner from the meeting space. You said something about how this was a combination of Anne Lamott and Gurumayi. It took me a few seconds to understand what you were saying, feeling. It's the few seconds that are relevant here—that it isn't automatic or natural for me to understand. This has been happening for years—that I will (it will happen tonight, for instance, when I enter the shoe room) walk into the room where people are waiting, and I'll realize from their faces, voices, and body posture that they are relating to me as if I'm special, and there's always this "huh?" in me. It isn't anything like false humility. It takes a few seconds for me to "go to them," to imagine what they're experiencing and to account for it. And I just now understood something, why I am never noticing what the other person may be feeling, in this regard. For me, whatever is going on is so radically non-personal, so huge, that I experience it as if it has nothing at all to do with "me." It's more like "we are all in It together." Yes, I'm aware that I am able to "enable the atmosphere," and I don't discount the value of that. But when I/we are in it, it's so profoundly non-personal that I've lost all awareness of myself. So it's always a bit of a surprise when I notice somebody thinking I'm special. When you said that about dependence on me, I had to work to understand. Just like in Novato.

It seems there is some process in your orientation to me, some lovely falling-apart of something that's no longer needed. Maybe a door opens to whatever can now be possible. Who knows? Mystery abounds. As things fall away from you (that dependence, the sense of obligation to call P. by a certain time, habits, and patterns of all sorts), realize that they had their usefulness for a time. New things will come to you, and they too will be useful for some period of time, eventually opening the door to whole new realizations, and then new fallings-away. It won't end.

Love,

Jan

DECEMBER 14TH, 2013

Dear Jan,

Oh, my Jan, such blessings and gratitude. I think I might burst, except there is more and more room to play.

So further reflections: emptiness/awareness sees itself through these eyes. "I" am the reflected and the reflector; the sky, the leather of a purse, the mannerisms of this person speaking, the wind caressing the tall grasses. Yesterday I awoke tired and sad—I had many things that had to be done—wrapping and mailing Christmas presents to my grandsons in Madrid, doing some accounting so I could pay my estimated taxes, and on and on. I felt tired, sad, and burdened most of the day. What was interesting though is that how I felt didn't show up as a story or complaint, nor did it stir up any fear or anxiety, just a lack of resistance to what was. So I was tired and sad.

Today I woke up happy—with a completely open day ahead. I reveled in a hike, cutting up vegetables, and taking a nap in the direct 3:00 p.m. sunlight coming through the bedroom window. Again, no story involved. I prefer the happy state and yet, as Rumi reveals in his poetry, there is room for any guest to show up, depression, anger, sorrow, and so on.

But what is so striking is how everything, everything simply comes and goes! Last evening I had dinner with J.—there appears to be a gradual ease with long-term friends—at least that was true last night. There is a difference in how open I am, meaning there was an ongoing awareness of the difference and the sameness between us and yet, I was able to speak a bit more freely about what it is like from these eyes, all the while being engaged with where she is. One of the interesting moments came when we were talking about consciousness and she said that the important thing is to be connected to consciousness. I spontaneously said, "we are consciousness." Not only did that allow me to be more forthcoming, it also opened the door to see, taste, and appreciate the difference between the illusion of separate consciousness and the reality of unity consciousness. In the moment with vivid clarity how can we not be connected to consciousness; and how impossible it was when I was asleep to see anything different, no matter how well intentioned or interested.

I read a *New Yorker* article on police tactics for getting people to falsely confess to crimes they did not commit and was reminded of how easily persuaded and conditioned we humans are. And since emptiness is revealing itself these days I mused, hmm. . . we are emptiness and therefore, can and are programmed with whatever is in our field, especially, being asleep, not paying attention, being a child, or being particularly susceptible or believing that we are separate. We are, in fact, pure vapor. Wow, maybe this is partly what you mean by mindful awareness! Compelling place to continue this wondering.

And one other thing before I call it a night: having lived most of my early life dissociated I continually questioned how people could possibly, really believe in the lives they were living. Between that dynamic and feeling fierce about discovering what was true/real I lived "outside" most of human interactions and the world. Keeping in mind I was humbled to find where and how I also fell into the traps of believing, I am struck these days at how that was a helpful training ground for genuine detachment and realizing the profound illusion of this world. In that way, it is so familiar and comfortable and home. It's fun to look back and see all the glimpses of what is right there.

And on that note I will call it a night.

Tons of love, Jan.

Beth

December 15th, 2013

What you said about childhood dissociation is so interesting, Beth.

I immediately saw what you were suggesting. It reminds me of things Eckhart has said about living/traveling in several cultures, different from one's own, and also about being gay. How these things (anything, really) that interfere with the standard definition of the norm, or that call attention to what is "just" identification—how they can prepare the ground for a loose sense of self, and so leave open possibility that might not be there so much for someone who lives as the norm, deeply identified. And I think of anybody with extreme physical limitation or disfigurement, who must surely know early on that they are not their bodies (or else live lives of terrible despair and anger).

It's just so strange that something (like cerebral palsy, like sexual abuse) universally seen to be unfortunate could somehow end up being a door-opener.

I'd be very glad to talk with you between Christmas and New Year's. We can check in as the time gets closer and see about the when of it.

It's very cold here. Below zero, I think, or at least it was overnight. With this glorious bright moon.

What you said, about J., the post-reflection, and your reading what you did in the David Carse book—maybe that will come up when we talk. I'm interested in exploring that with you. The business of us all being one and yet (clearly) in different places, and when something comes to you to say, or not (in response to what she said about consciousness).

I am just loving this time I'm in. So many long stretches of quiet, stillness. I have been getting out a little, some fun stuff, mostly to do with music, a little with friends.

Great love to you,

Jan

* * *

I began a correspondence with a young man and I have included my portion of our "conversation"—each time I write about the shift it has more dimension to it.

DECEMBER 14TH, 2013

Hello,

Greetings from San Francisco. There is so much awe and wonder in everyday life. . .

In so many ways I feel newly born, seeing everything through such different eyes, even though everything is exactly the same.

Today I awoke early and went for a long leisurely walk/hike in one of my favorite spots (north of the city), came home to take a rest with the afternoon sun pouring through the window, and had a phone conversation with a cousin. I washed vegetables to prepare for a salad for dinner.

In other words, pretty ordinary and familiar.

And yet . . . there is a vast joy and emptiness permeating everything, sometimes to bursting. As the personality, slowly but surely, continues to empty out, taking with it anxieties, opinions, and illusions of control, a sense of awe, happiness, ease, and fluidity pours in and around. I am beginning to see how this consciousness/

emptiness we are moves, moves as life happens. And the emptiness reflects all. Amazing.

I am adjusting to the profound shift; going along for the ride so to speak. And considering that everything is included, meaning I don't turn away from anything seen or felt, there are challenging moments. The other thing, here, that is so different though, is nothing sticks. It all shows up, challenging and not, and it all moves on. Such contrast to the period of devoted surrendering (and even more of a contrast to a lifetime of suffering).

Warmly,

Beth

* * *

Hello,

Happy holidays to you and your family . . . it is a stunningly clear (and warm) day here in San Francisco.

I have been sitting in quiet amongst a grove of eucalyptus trees, enjoying the butterflies and crows.

And wondering where I would enter the field of rebirth—the moment itself was so gentle and simple it still seems a marvel; like you said so simply there all along.

We were in a retreat . . . there were eight people sitting with Jan for three full days, oh, the very wonder of it. We were in a private home in the hills of Marin County (outside of San Francisco) with lots of floor to ceiling windows so the beauty of nature was at our fingertips. It was Thursday afternoon, nearing the end of our time together and I remember thinking, wouldn't it be fabulous to wake up in the midst of people! Whatever that might have meant at the time! We went into a visualization (perhaps you are familiar with the elevator, going up, down, left, right, etc., that Jan uses in her retreats—it was that one) that struck very deeply, very deeply in fact; in the sense that I could actually feel the spontaneous opening, the complete opening, of the solar plexus. My entire body filled with heat, a lot of heat, feeling like the body was completely burning up—very hot, but not particularly uncomfortable. I think I began to sweat, realizing this was a visible happening, a real

172

happening; and it is only in reflection that I know now that I was no more. Again, so profoundly quiet and simple, like a soft wind blew a flimsy veil from my eyes. And said, "see, how natural this is and see how it's always been right there, really right there."

When I opened my eyes and looked around the room I was positively overcome with love—could hardly contain it, and had no idea what to "do" with all the outpouring. I slowly looked at everyone in the room and, again, simply and almost matter-of-factly saw no separation. There being no separation anywhere appeared as a of-course-ness; what still blew me out of the water was how gentle and kind the happening was.

Being able to express the intensity of love took many, many tries that afternoon. It was so big and unabashed it felt like giving birth—which I guess you could say it was! I remember Jan saying God bless and feeling that somehow she was registering the significance of this seemingly simple moment!

And the really funny part . . . I did not recognize it that afternoon. I had a long visit with Jan that evening; we sat together for a couple of hours talking, soaking up presence and being-ness and I drove home very tired and happy. The next day it hit me like a ton of bricks. I get weepy remembering the very moment when it dawned on me, and feeling giddy, positively giddy. I walked down to a neighboring street to get some food and realized wow—everything is exactly the same and everything is completely different. Awareness was looking out of these eyes! Awareness sees people walking up and down Fillmore Street. Awareness sees the trees, the electrical lines, this store at this corner, and that store, at that one.

And came home to write to Jan . . . "did you know? Could you tell?"

I had been working with Jan for about a year by then . . . by phone for many months and then in person. I flew to Vermont to spend a week with her last January. . . knowing in some intuitive way that being is contagious and that putting myself into the field of presence as much as possible would allow recognition to burst forward.

I think I will leave this part (the time with her and the process of surrendering) of the journey for another time. I am tired and getting ready to fly to Florida to spend some time with a beloved aunt who is in the process of dying.

Warmly,

Beth

* * *

Hello,

Greetings again from San Francisco.

I thought of you today as I went about my business and realized how giddy and happy I am—for no reason at all. I wonder if you have similar moments/days. Merely being alive . . . something that would have made no real sense to me "before." No matter what happens, no matter how I am feeling, it is simply a matter of being "it" from moment to moment. Life moving through this body . . . so peaceful and free, free of effort.

Which brings me to surrender—at the risk of making something really non-understandable and profoundly mysterious, I'll delve into what it has been like. On one hand, over the last few years there was an increasing awareness, in a very real sense, of love, something vast, present, and what could only be known as awesome and divine. I read Adyashanti, talked with Jan, immersed in various other awakened souls, all the while deepening into what I knew I already knew. On the other hand, I was plagued by visions and gut-wrenching terrors coming from "seeing" myself at the edge of a chasm. My awareness of the ego/mind not being real grew, going from an intellectual understanding to a knowing, a real knowing; almost like a science project, watching the Petri dish reveal its secrets. Which, I am guessing, is how come I was afraid. I remember, even with humor, saying to myself, "it's okay, I know it's scary to die, it's scary and it's going to happen."

All the while, a continual prayer of "Thy Will Be Done" and a deepening alignment with what is true, no matter what!

Sometimes the fear of the "Grand Canyon" as I began to call it, was abstract and amorphous, and sometimes it was right in my face . . . willingly letting go of being right or heard or willingly taking in the other person who I was angry with. More often than not, my workout came in the form of relationships.

All the while going deeper and deeper into knowing the mind's chatter is not real and one day having the vision of the Grand Canyon and realizing I had already jumped—to think there was any deliberation left was a joke!

And somewhere in here, diving to a pretty rock bottom place of my mind and seeing, boldly and without any filters that everything I had ever done was to be loved and taken care of. Without judgment seeing the totality of that motivation, and only that motivation, meaning not a moment of authenticity over my lifetime. Nothing real. It rocked me and liberated me all at the same time because it was humbling and true, and because there was so much compassion for what it is like to be human.

Jumping now to "after" the complete shift in perspective (the retreat with Jan) I was awakened in the middle of the night with a spontaneous vision: a vision of falling or walking off the cliff, this time seeing the sheer reality of all/everything being consciousness and watching as the "form" fell from the edge and dissolved, gently and simply back into its original nothingness, and there simply was no splat. Only vapor to vapor, love into love, being into being. There is no death. The image seemed a bit one dimensional and over time I am aware of how I am settling into that being the truth and very real.

Also, in two weeks I am going to Mt. Arunachula—India—for a three week retreat—This is the mountain Ramana Maharshi lived on for most of his life. There will be lots of silence, satsangs, and time to walk around the mountain and be with the silence. I am pretty darned excited!

I think I will stop here and let things simmer while I send it off to you.

Until next time,
Beth

"I did what thousands of pilgrims through the ages have done before me and will do after: I praised the God of Light and asked for liberation in this life, so as to serve God in this body."

ANDREW HARVEY
The Hidden Journey

I had felt a call to India for decades. I couldn't have told you why or even what I might have expected, only that it seemed "a foregone conclusion" that I would some day travel there.

The "invitation" made itself real and in present time when I read about Yukio Ramana, an awakened being who, having studied with a dearly loved teacher, Papaji, led pilgrimages to the sacred mountain, Mt. Arunachala. He specialized in bringing westerners to the colorful, seemingly chaotic, and at-first-appearing-confusing life in India. Inside a local ashram he invited people to come be with the mountain—sit in its shadow, walk its circumference, walk to the summit, sit in the caves, meditate, and meet with local awakened souls. I am unfamiliar with the mountain and only have a fleeting exposure to Ramana Maharshi, but I feel pulled and excited so say yes to the adventure, wholeheartedly.

The plane ride is over nineteen hours long and the car ride from the airport to the ashram is five hours during the middle of the night. I am exhilarated the entire journey *(I cannot help but notice that I am not frightened)*. My first impressions of India are one of constant movement. Everything and everyone is alive. Even in the middle of the night, people are walking, shopping, and visiting. Our driver passes trucks, buses, cars, bikes, and motorcycles, honking his horn over and over again, not as an annoyance, but as a notice that he is passing—coming within inches of the vehicle in front. And so we speed through the night and I am quickly aware that there is a rhythm to this stream of movement—one I will witness and settle deeper into over time.

MOUNT ARUNACHALA

I literally gasp when, upon turning around on the second floor of the ashram, jet-lagged and weary, having lugged my suitcase up the stairs on my way to my room, I get my first up-close glimpse of the mountain. It is pulsating with life and profound silence. I feel speechless and aware of the pure delight of having been taken so by surprise—the surprise of impact. And for the recognition—the sweet and unambiguous, undeniable recognition of an awake mountain.

Our first evening there, after meeting and breaking bread with the others who have made this anticipated journey—people from around the world, Poland, Hong Kong, Canada, and different states in the U.S.—we get together for a Puja ceremony. A first for me and I am enchanted. We gather in a small room, snugly sitting facing an adorned altar, with statues and colorful materials, all in keeping with a reverence to Hindu gods and goddesses. If and when we feel so moved we are invited to walk up to Ramana and his wife who are flanking the altar, welcoming us to a reverential surrender. We are invited to let go—to listen to our depths and respond from there. I walk slowly, in and amongst the legs and arms of my fellow travelers, and, with tremendous, but quiet, enthusiasm I prostrate myself in front of the altar. I have not had any previous experience with bowing, and yet I completely bow in full-on devotion. The feeling inside me is *I cannot get flat enough*—like I have been doing this my whole life and it is the most natural thing in the world, to give everything, to completely give over, to "I offer anything and everything," I hold nothing back. I silently pray, tears streaming down my face. A private and full devotion to whatever it takes to be, to be ever and ever fully realized, to an ever-unfolding transparency.

There is an intuitive knowing here—transcendence, waking up to reality continues. And, without it being a fully conscious awareness, this moment of offering everything and anything harkens back to an earlier time when I hesitated from fully letting go—when the sentry showed up and, in the name of protection, stopped the dissolution—leaving a trace.

JANUARY 30TH, 2014

A couple of days after the Puja ceremony I meet Ramana on the veranda of the second floor of the ashram for a private session, one he requires of everyone joining him on the retreat. I sit on the futon, facing the mountain and he hooks me up to a biofeedback machine, a clip on my ear and a clip on a finger. He has designed a beautiful and effective process to help people release "stuff" and open to a larger reality. He is able to monitor our resonance, with the machine. He can measure when our body's response indicates a dropping into a clearer and more direct perspective.

In the session I am taken through a series of releases—releasing held patterns and constrictions. All the while opening to the deeper reality through perceptual shifts of awareness. With Ramana's guidance, and in my mind's eye, I am looking and seeing through softer eyes—seeing things as they really are—not working hard or distorting. And experiencing the vastness of space, space from which everything arises, experiencing it by opening to its presence in and around all, in, around, and through everything.

With my eyes closed I can actually experience the vastness, 360 degrees around me.

And, with Ramana's pointing, I profoundly sink into a direct perception of the unending, vibrating, soft effervescence of presence. I completely sink into direct awareness. And dissolve.

There are no words. Literally, no words.

There is immense and unending gratitude.

FEBRUARY 1ST, 2014

Dearest Jan,

The warmest of greetings to you from Mt. Arunachala. I am sitting on my very simple (and hard) cot at the end of the day. There are many, many things I could tell you about . . . And I will when I get home.

Except the moment. Beginning with a fire burning fiercely in my heart (very similar to the moment with you in Mill Valley when a fire cleansed and opened my gut).

And then an opening of perception (a direct knowing of) forever and beyond. Pure vastness that has no beginning or end. Pure space that is magnificence itself. An emptiness that is achingly full. And there is no me. Nothing.

And . . . today awareness moved through the day delighting in all. You are deep in my heart.

Love,

Beth

* * *

Any attempt to "capture" or describe what was revealed falls flat and inconsequential. Was it what is there (and always has been) when all the veils drop off? A direct knowing, a close, intimate direct knowing of what we are. As "I" sat there, eyes closed, sitting in the silence of the mountain, having the universe reveal itself, the vast, vast emptiness pulsating with life, teeming with formless life, in all perpetuity, profoundly alive, soft, and gentle. Watching as this "I" diminishes, dissolves, and completely disappears into the emptiness of all there is.

Not a trace left and even more astonishing is the smallness, the mere speck of the "I" as, when it disappears, leaves not a trace. I am simply not able to convey the "magnitude" of this gone-ness. And yet, I try—the entire form dissolving, fully and completely disappearing into the indescribable magnificence of the eternal.

I am not able to fully grasp the amazement, nor the gratitude of being in the midst of "yes, yes, finally and fully home." It is overwhelming in the most glorious way.

The vessel held and the vessel dissolved.

I sat for hours, outside my room, in full view of the mountain, my feet on the balcony, hardly moving. I watched the mosquitoes land on my flesh and watched the bites come and go. I cried and cried, without an inkling of why. I lived in a refrain of "oh my, oh my, oh my" for days on end. Sometimes the cries came from deep inside my belly, and I sobbed and sobbed.

Many of us walked through the fields of India, amongst trash, rubble, grasses, and cows, to a nearby home, to join a *Kirtan*—a call and response chanting—a deeply devotional Bhakti tradition. I stood in the back of the room and I can't really say I listened because it felt more like being in and of the music. And I continued to cry, tears wetting my cheeks, my body swaying, as the beauty of this ancient recognition of opening your heart to the sounds of the universe.

Some part of me was aware of being completely un-self-conscious and of how novel that was.

It was sweltering hot and a swirl of colors, odors, and commotion. I loved the rhythms, the cars, cows, monkeys, motorcycles, buses, bikes, dogs, cats, and people all sharing the streets and the roads. It seemed that everything was in some state of disrepair and the electricity went off for hours at a time. I learned to respect the local monkeys who showed up everywhere and "thought" nothing of jumping out at you if you had something they wanted to eat. My first day there, emptying my pail (no toilet paper allowed in the toilets!) into the outside dumpster . . . the lid up higher than my head, having me step on an accompanying brick, I came face to face with a monkey as he jumped out of the dumpster when I lifted the lid.

I was aware of being surprised . . . and not frightened. This would have freaked me out "before."

We were invited to sit with awakened folks who lived in and around the area. Ramana took the group to a few different satsangs and we were free to go back if so moved. I went to Siva/Shakti Amman's gathering three times and truth be told could have stayed there forever.

Siva/Shakti is a tiny woman, wrapped in a colorful sari. Her satsangs are conducted in silence. The room fills beyond capacity a good half hour before she is expected to arrive, people coming in and finding a spot on the floor, or a few chairs located around the periphery. The hustle and bustle of settling in is the only sound in the room. The silence holds center stage. Siva/Shakti quietly floats into the room, like a breeze that hardly moves anything in its presence but nonetheless is felt as everything around it shifts.

My first visit I am sitting on a cushion with my back against the wall. There isn't a square inch of floor space not taken up by a body, sitting motionless on a yoga cushion, and as I sit there I am aware of the chest-high windows that run across the side and back walls of the building. People are walking along the outside path, finding an inch of window to stand by, peering into the room, hoping for a glimpse of Siva/Shakti.

She walks into the room and sits on a chair, situated in the center of our horseshoe circle. She is profoundly quiet, deeply and compellingly still. She sits and lets her eyes gaze over the crowd. Her eyes stopping here and there to soak in—look deeply into a person's eyes.

I am profoundly aware of being in the midst of the radiance of God. Here is what radiance looks like in human form. With nary a word . . . no, in fact, it could not be spoken of . . . it is present; it is palpable in pure stillness. The face of God's radiance. Palpably palpable. I want to say out loud . . . "put out your hand, touch, open your lips and taste; it's right here." And it abides in humanity.

I sit the half-hour in reverence.

The next time I go I sit in a chair at the back wall; a different perspective on the room. This time, as Siva/Shakti arrives, sits down, and scans the faces in the room, gets up and slowly walks closer to folks, taking in, drinking in, the upturned, longing faces, I am more aware of the folks crowding the windows from outside the building. Noses pressed against the bars on the windows, hands curled around the bars, heads turned in order to see more deeply into the room—eyes following Siva's movements. The room and the path around the building are teeming with folks and I am, in my mind's eye, transported to biblical times. Jesus is preaching to the multitudes and people are hanging from trees, bunched into doorways, squinting into windows, attempting to get a glimpse, receive a blessing, to be uplifted by an awakened being. The presence in this room is one and the same—there is no distinction in time—it is all happening in this very moment.

I feel at home in this environment—a sense of familiarity and ease—Jesus is alive in "me." Am "I" right here as he is teaching? Here is oneness! That is how real it is to me. Many years before this trip I was in Jerusalem and was moved to tears as I traced different places that Jesus had walked, talked with his disciples, and was crucified. I sat in the garden of Gethsemane and wept for something I could not comprehend. I am aware of a lifetime of being compelled by Jesus' crucifixion, not being able to find the essence of what recognition it was revealing. Years later I read Andrew Harvey in *Hidden Journey*—and "got it!"

"Every human being has to say in the end what Christ said at Gethsemane: Not my will but your will, and when that yes is said the doors of Death and Illusion crumble."

This is the dying before dying. This is the essence of living true.

The third time I went to Siva/Shakti's satsang I once again sat in a chair, this time against the wall at the side of the building that is closest to the door, giving me a view of the people filling in to sit with her. I am there early and watch as the room fills up and I see helpers silently gesture to folks sitting on the floor to please move closer together, making more room for other bodies to fit. I see a young man sitting close to the door. A woman asks him to please move further over and he becomes quite agitated. His face is strained and obviously upset. He is near tears and unhappily gets up and moves his cushion closer to the person on his right. The incident is over quickly but his upset is not. He is visibly distraught and fighting tears as people moving around him settle in to wait for Siva/Shakti to arrive.

She walks in, sits down, and then begins her slow walk around the front of the room. I watch as she meets the gaze of some, staying with them for a bit of time, moving onto someone else. All eyes, if open, are holding her tightly in their gaze. As I watch her move along, sometimes holding a hand out towards a person, I become aware that she is picking up on pain and suffering in particular folks. From where I am sitting the encounter between them seems unmistakable. From vast, silent oneness, she is transmitting peace and powerful presence.

The young man who is still agitated is sitting next to the door— the one where she will exit, having scanned the entire room by that time. I am between her and this man, facing him. I am able to see his face as she stops in front of him and stands still, completely still. She holds his gaze and I watch as his face crumbles into her gaze, the stress and tension melting from his face and out of his body. There is a vast steady current of quiet love as they gaze into each other's eyes. A deep, abiding silence fills the room with a palpable sense of deep longing and love. He begins to cry, tears running steadily down his face as his worries collapse. I am watching as this young man is moved to let go and visibly look peaceful, moved, and grateful. I sit and watch as tears travel down my cheeks. And there is no separation between him and me, no separation between Siva/Shakti and me, no separation between the bars of the windows and me. One tear, one gaze, one soul. It is pure radiance that is filling my body, looking out my eyes, and opening our hearts as the beloved.

And Siva/Shakti leaves the room—the silence left in her wake.

The grace of being in India showed me the grace of pure being, uninhibited, completely unself-conscious, not "owing" anyone a "pretend" encounter. My meals were provided; I wasn't responsible for anyone else's well-being or needs, I was emptied of effort: India, the mountain, and awakened beings were all available, keeping me in a steady state of expanded awareness and bliss. The unrelenting heat, the hungry mosquitoes, the rubble of the streets, the buildings, the unreliable electricity, fans, ATM machines, the cow giving birth on a side street, the magnificent ascent and descent of the mountain, the eight mile walk around the mountain, all in the name of surrendering whatever was keeping us from true freedom. I sat in the caves on the mountain and met the real presence of Ramana Maharshi himself enough times that I began to feel a deep familiarity and delight when he showed up and stayed long enough for a chat. His presence is palpable; I encountered the outline of his human form a couple of times, no words passing between us, but a simple recognition—one time, as I lay quietly on my cot, waiting for sleep, in the aftermath of a fellow devotee having had a stroke, and the other sitting in the "mother's cave," looking out the sole tiny window, encountering him face-to-face, bringing a deep smile throughout my body. The Hindu ceremonies in nearby temples, the abiding immersion in the atmosphere of devotion and inquiry into our true nature...

"*Now I was home, alone, surrounded by everything I loved the most. I could go mad into (Life) and dance and play (and cry) with (Devotion) far away from the world, far away from all . . . inhibition . . . live the ecstasy with complete abandon and far from anyone I knew.*"

ANDREW HARVEY
The Hidden Journey

* * *

BACK HOME
BUBBLING OVER
MARCH 28TH, 2014

Reporting this cannot possibly begin to say it, not really, cannot understand what it really means, if it means anything at all.

And yet, say it I will. I am overwhelmed with love and devotion. I lay prone, spread out, flat on the ground, opening, opening, opening.

I am conditioned, as a Jew, to not bow to anything or anyone, and yet this is the most natural gesture. Possibly one of the most natural in my life

To bow deeply

To bow fully

To surrender and love

And give everything

And give anything

Anything and everything that is asked for

To be truth

To be love

To be what we are

What I am

I am going through the motions of everyday life, on the surface being with my family, sitting with my patients, watching a TV program.

I am aware of being well-conditioned for living with a hidden secret, holding back the sheer immensity, my god the sheer immensity. What can I really say to describe this fullness? The fullness is pressing and seems to promise to push open through my heart and chest and dissolve me into the glory and grandeur of the ineffable.

Oh, to be able to use simple words . . . words that can be seen, heard, touched.

Like a dam bursting.

Oh my, oh my.

It must be spoken . . . a leaky valve pressure is building up—pushing release, release.

Tears, so many tears
Of pure happiness
And gratitude—oh my goodness, such profound gratitude.
How deeply can I bow?
How prostrate can I lie?
How deep into the earth can I burrow to sing my love and my thanks?
Like Tutankhamun, I feel unbelievable joy and gratitude for finding what I always knew was there and was real.

Throughout my lifetime, the small quiet voice questioned the way we humans were living, thinking, and believing. I couldn't honestly invest in any of it, but how I tried, dear god, how I tried.

I had been living in "two worlds" with a profound lifetime of longing and being so confused at times. Longing for what? For belonging in this world or being loved by someone special?

And that quiet knowing . . . there is something deeper, something I "remember," something deeper that is cut off, deeper than mother, lover, friend, deeper than this world.

Listen to Rumi . . .

THE REED FLUTE'S SONG

Listen to the story told by the reed,
of being separated.

185

"Since I was cut from the reedbed,
I have made this crying sound.

Anyone apart from someone he loves
understands what I say.

Anyone pulled from a source
longs to go back.

At any gathering I am there,
mingling in the laughing and grieving,

a friend to each, but few
will hear the secrets hidden

within the notes. No ears for that.
Body flowing out of spirit,

spirit up from body: no concealing
that mixing. But it's not given us

to see the soul. The reed flute
is fire, not wind. Be that empty."

Hear the love fire tangled
in the reed notes, as bewilderment

melts into wine. The reed is a friend
to all who want the fabric torn

and drawn away. The reed is hurt
and salve combining. Intimacy

and longing for intimacy, one
song. A disastrous surrender

186

and a fine love, together. The one
who secretly hears this is senseless.

A tongue has one customer, the ear.
A sugarcane flute has such effect

because it was able to make sugar
in the reedbed. The sound it makes

is for everyone. Days full of wanting,
let them go by without worrying

that they do. Stay where you are
inside such a pure, hollow note.

Every thirst gets satisfied except
that of these fish, the mystics,

who swim a vast ocean of grace
still somehow longing for it!

No one lives in that without
being nourished every day.

But if someone doesn't want to hear
the song of the reed flute,

it's best to cut conversation
short, say good-bye, and leave.

COLEMAN BARKS TRANSLATION
The Essential Rumi

Ramana Maharshi is real to me . . .

He is as real to me as sitting down to dinner together, in elegant silence.

Jesus is real to me . . .

Bowing to a beloved master in the flesh and blood.

I commune with both . . .

Some would say I have fallen off the deep end and I'd say that is probably true. Fallen into a love for life—all of life—every little bit of it . . .

I listen to a favorite spiritual chant, full of deep juicy devotion . . . to the narcissist, the blue jay, the gurgling river, the sun, the moon, and to Mount Arunachala.

And I see the divine is manifested in everything, every molecule, every cell, mysteriously so, including the person you hate, the abuse you endured, and the unbearable loss.

Our human being-ness, this human life appears, in so many ways, mysterious. It does seem that we have the possibility and the potential for increasing consciousness while we are here. It does seem that the opening and increasing consciousness is in the service of waking us to our true natures—to know ourselves as pure awareness, oneness.

We live on a planet of duality. In the conditioned state of perceived separation, every one of us is immersed in the belief of this and that, right and wrong, good and bad, me and you, inside and outside. Mostly we find ways of attributing the fault, blame, and "badness" to someone or something else, attempting to reassure ourselves that we are safe, we are secure.

The density of that belief seems to be in alignment with our level of consciousness. And how strongly we are identified with our apparent structure—our bodies, our minds, our personalities. The more conscious we are of our inner state and our impact on the world, the more transparent we are, the less judgmental we are. Conversely, the less conscious we are the denser we are, the louder our protests.

* * *

Freedom is living life as it is; a deep joy in meeting others, and life as it is in each moment.

The spaciousness . . . oh my, the spaciousness! Space—loneliness, if it is even present is so rare these days—rests.

There is no sense in looking for something in the future when it is right here now.

I look back and see the "work" it took to surrender over and over, to surrender to what is true right now.

The "work," the practice, was whatever it took to allow the surrender so that perception could shift. It was the willingness to see through the conditioned mind, the conditioned beliefs, and the insistence of my ego's belief in itself as reality. It was seeing this over and over, and more deeply. The practice was surrendering the conditioned illusion of control. It was surrendering illusion after illusion. It was welcoming disillusionment.

Insights and knowing show up like faceted jewels shining in a night sky.

The true Self resonates in my bones, it absolutely recognizes itself.

Look here, right here, now, not out there.

Living without attachment or some insistence as to how it should be is freedom to fully enjoy what is.

Ease and acceptance are grounded in experientially knowing.

Recognition of its continuation, its constancy.

High Indifference (Franklin Merrill-Wolff). It doesn't matter what happens. It really doesn't matter. At the very same time there is a deep love and caring for all who suffer.

Silence is freed and permeates everything.

Truth recognizes truth.

The inner teacher is always awake.

"All goes onward and outward, nothing collapses.
And to die is different from what any one supposed, and luckier."

WALT WHITMAN

My cup runneth over. I discover, over and over, the exquisiteness of the ordinary, and the moment of what is.

APRIL 5TH, 2014

I am noticing that creativity is abundantly available. By living without resistance, fear, or protest, spontaneous creativity is at my fingertips more and more.

I leave for work and discover the garage door is broken. I park in a two-car garage with two separate doors, one for each car. Fortunately my neighbor has already left. Using his entry into the garage I get in my car and with careful maneuverings I drive my car up and back, a little to the left and a little to the right until I manage, in a very tight space, to back out the neighbor's garage door.

I am on my way to work within minutes of discovering my broken door, with much rejoicing inside. I cannot help but notice how different this is from "before" when worry and manufactured stories about "whatever" would have taken up all the stage and energy.

There is a common worry/question amongst seekers that without the mind planning/controlling, solving worrisome problems, and orchestrating activity we would cease to care, be engaged, able to work, parent, or contribute to society. But, the creativity, the energy, the intelligence that is available when the conditioned mind and body are retired is far beyond anything our puny small selves can possibly even imagine much less manifest.

APRIL 22ND, 2014

I am sad. My beloved aunt has passed away. I am grateful for our last visit, just the two of us enjoying each other's company, knowing this would be the last time we saw each other. We laughed and went out to dinner and the movies; we reminisced and shared some sorrows. She told me about being a young girl and swimming too far out into the ocean. As she remembered it, she believed she was going to die and wasn't afraid. She said she was ready to die now, as well.

When it was time for me to leave her home and go to the airport, the Uber driver only minutes away from picking me up, we said goodbye. I was moved and touched and, frankly, a bit astonished, that she held my gaze the entire time. We had had a deep affection for each other, no matter how long we might have gone without seeing each other and now we were parting for good. Love held us as we drank each other in and said our final farewell. I am grateful for our direct goodbye, neither one of us looking away from the truth of this leave-taking.

And now, I am deeply sad. I adore her.

APRIL 24TH, 2014

I have a sense of losing my mind but with great joy. Vastness is flowing in more and more, expanding. This is being in every moment without thinking, choosing, or planning. Each moment is so big.

APRIL 27TH, 2014

My heart is breaking. I feel deep sadness, and I miss my aunt. I watch as my heart opens and breaks further into the truth of this loss.

There is ruthless self-honesty, which deepens the rootedness in truth. There is total alignment with life, responding appropriately to whatever is rising. I am more and more comfortable with responding spontaneously, even if and when it might be upsetting to another, or upsetting the image I had held of myself.

This gets my attention, especially, in the wake of a lifetime of holding back on what I think, feel, and want. Life, in and of itself, speaks and acts of its own volition, and with honesty and kindness.

Life is serving itself in every moment in every which way.

MAY 5TH, 2014

I am noticing there is more automatic generosity as I move through the days. I am noticing the absence of a mental state of self-involvement and guardedness. I feel spontaneously moved to offer whatever might be offered in the moment. I am sitting in a coffee shop and a mother is impatient, yelling at her four-year old who is bored and restless. It is jarring to sit next to them. It is harsh, as if, from her point of view, he is the very cause of her foul mood.

"Don't sit on the floor!" "You almost knocked over my coffee." "You are being a pain in the neck." "You almost knocked over my coffee." She says this several times, without moving her coffee cup out of the way. She loses her patience over and over, and the child asks over and over to leave and go home. I sit for a while, wondering what games I might have on my computer that would interest him, wishing I had a deck of cards with me, and finally turn to the child and ask him if he is bored and whether he knows how to play I Spy. His eyes light up and I see his mother relax. I spy something blue—a mailbox several yards away. We play for a while and all of us are more at ease, when they get up to leave. "That was a hard one," he tells me.

Yes, it was definitely hard—probably impossible for him to know what was going on, why he was being yelled at, what might make his mother happy, what might make him happy. And for his mother, it was also probably very hard. What was really bothering her, and what might have helped? How would she feel if she recognized how her upset was affecting her son, affecting her? When they get up to leave the coffee shop, both mother and child are relaxed and smiling.

I am aware of how differently I responded. Typically I would have been triggered and bothered. I most likely would have felt helpless in the face of such harshness and ended up being angry with the mother. But now, without any thought or effort I diffuse the situation. But the truth be known, "I" didn't do anything. This is how it goes now that creativity, life, intelligence, love moves through this body and mind.

MAY 9TH, 2014

And now, I am sitting in sorrow, experiencing anguish. An old record is playing in my head. I feel wounded and caught inside my head. At some level, in some cell of my being I fell back into believing I am separate and alone. Life/awareness is experiencing itself in human form—noticing, watching.

The machinery that is my mind, so, so used to doing its job of navigating the world is sputtering along. In its wildness, in its conditioned state it is both habitual and alluring. Like the circus elephant, accustomed to being shackled and in chains, does not easily or quickly recognize its freedom when the shackles are removed.

And yet, here is the formless, the source of all, the all-pervasive force of love, seeing the movement of form, the movement of human conditioning, and the movement of unconditional love— even, and maybe even especially, for the wounds, confusion, and the habits of the human mind.

MAY 25TH, 2014

I am the energizer bunny . . . and cannot get over the difference here. Energy abounds, today there is a steady stream of energy. It is moving to me. I go to the farmer's market, have brunch with friends, get the car washed, go the grocery store and put the groceries away, I read the paper, go to the local coffee shop and read, I put on music and cook for the week, I watch TV, empty the dishwasher, write, and hang a wall-hanging in the communal laundry room.

I do all of this with enormous ease and engagement. Again, there is rejoicing inside. It feels like a miracle, having been living in a frightened, paralyzed state of self-protection for most of my life.

JUNE 10TH, 2014

I appear to be sinking further and further into the natural state of awareness . . . with a feeling of greater and more profound indifference.

JUNE 15TH, 2014

Truth experiences itself in different ways.
There is a direct encounter:
Formless – I am everything
Form – personal body and mind, made up of history and memories
Beyond – indescribable

In this there is a freedom for being to move itself in and out of each of these states of consciousness.

JUNE 16TH, 2014

"I know that the spirit of God is the brother of my own."

WALT WHITMAN

I am reminded of being at Mt. Arunachala. A veil, with one intelligent caress, is torn from the eyes of the mind, letting the sight pierce through.

JUNE 20TH, 2014

There is a gathering process, allowing all to be here.
I am deepening in immediacy.
I put the key into the ignition and nothing happens.
I "think about it" and feel nervous.
The reality—the battery is dead and I effortlessly call AAA.

JUNE 24TH, 2014

There is more ease and a natural allowance, even a welcoming of whatever is being seen and felt, of what needs to be conscious and burned off.

* * *

I am in my car, in line to get into Trader Joe's parking lot. I see a Hispanic woman and her daughter, probably around ten or so, standing close together at the edge of the parking lot exit. The mom is holding up a sign and they are obviously asking for help. As I wait in line I see their close interactions with each other and even some ease with what they are doing. They are wearing clean clothes and appear organized. I have never seen them before and they stand out in terms of homeless or down and out as well.

When I leave the lot after shopping I offer them money and the mom comes over to take it and say thank you. The child jumps up and down and both of them keep eye contact with me as my car slowly makes its way out of the lot. The child continues to look at me and smile and wave her hands. In the midst of traffic and the hub-bub of a busy intersection, there is genuine contact between us and I am overcome with emotion and have a hard time keeping eye contact with them, realizing I cannot dissolve into tears and drive my car at the same time.

That night, in bed, I am overcome with weeping. I feel sorrow for them and for our human condition of poverty—in every which way we can be poor and lacking.

JUNE 25TH, 2014

I cannot fall asleep and spend a long night aware of being very anxious. This is unusual. I have not felt anxiety, at all, since returning from India. I am anxious and aware of many other emotions—jealousy and lacking, to name a couple.

At some point in the wee hours I fall asleep long enough to dream:

A very unappealing and unattractive man has pushed his finger/hand into the flesh of my hip where I have been in pain for a while. He pushes hard, and I feel a lot of pain. He is standing very close to me and not only hurting me but also harassing me by being too close and touching me. I am vocal and active in telling him to stop touching me and pushing him away. He does not listen.

At some point I get enough distance from him and push my thumbs into his shoulders and he says, "stop touching me." I tell him, "yes, this is how it feels" and this is why he should stop.

The dream wakes me and begins a horrifying and terrifying descent into a black place inside. I am aware that I have completely lost the light and I am beyond despair. It is completely real and I am desperate and floundering.

I am put to mind of the Bible when Jacob wrestles with the angel, of Jesus on the cross, and Kali, the god of destruction.

I am inside, engulfed in nameless, absolute, complete, unmitigated fear. I am inside a boundless black. I am inside pure darkness, which is as indescribable as pure emptiness—completely still and deeply silent. It is pure, endless darkness, containing nothing else, as is the terror I feel, as I am aware of being completely at its mercy.

And, something is watching, witnessing, seeing. Some observer attended.

And the mechanism (the mind) I have used to understand and manage makes a vain effort to deal. In the floundering I look to surrender and feel a horror that I am being asked to surrender to being hurt, as in the dream. My mind can only come up with paltry understandings and silly explanations in the face of such profundity.

I look to acceptance of what is going on and I feel an enormous resistance. No matter where I turn there is darkness and I feel really scared and alone. I am in the throes of rage and hatred, my mind's reaction to this profound unknown. In some small way I am aware that I am trying very hard to comprehend something that is incomprehensible and terrifying.

And something watches, witnesses the mind work furiously, to no avail. The mind, the insubstantial flimsy conditioned mind cannot comprehend, influence, cope, or contain any of this. Cannot succeed in surviving or giving me what I think I want, not anywhere near these odds.

At some point I realize I am completely, darkly, and thoroughly confused. But the very second I become aware of confusion, I fall into that confusion, and into the awareness of the confusion, and it all simply lifts and there is a sweet neutral ease.

I am familiar with this confusion. The seemingly inconceivable bafflement of what happened to the light. In the constricted state of fear and fury the light appears to have disappeared. Since birth I have felt confused by so many things in this world (as I think many of us are). Why are we so unhappy? Why do we hurt each other? What do I do with my strong emotions? How can we get so, so lost in darkness?

Either that night or the next morning I am aware of many things. How completely epic this experience felt. Maybe expressing how mythical, biblical, and gigantic the experience of "separation" feels. How indigestible the experience of assumed abandonment is for us humans.

The human experience of believing we are separate and alone. Living as if we are cut off, profoundly alone and disconnected, abandoned by life itself, we distract ourselves to avoid the experience and knowing of this agony, this terror coming from our beliefs, and our limited understandings.

I am aware of the darkness of rage and of hatred, the depth and enormity of the terror; the human reactions to such an existential belief. I am aware of the light never having left, but in the human darkness I cannot see it. I am aware of the universality of this, of the reverberating trauma and the way this belief and this experience resonates in the human being. And I am now aware of what it is like to be completely open, fully present, to this experience—in the middle of the black night and alone.

I am aware of the despair in us humans to be so profoundly (seemingly) cut off from the light, from who we really are, from our very essence, from the source. I am aware of the confusion in every cell of my being.

This is not intellectual. The felt sense and knowing of this is petrifying, and yet it is liberating to see through the illusion, the veil, and the folly of believing we are alone and separate. And most amazing of all, once seen and felt, the terror and the illusion evaporates. Poof!

Sometime later, I more intensely resonated and experientially understood David Hawkins' telling of what looked to me a similar encounter:

"The ecstasy that accompanies this condition (Love of the Presence) isn't absolutely stable; keep in mind that there are also moments of great agony. The most intense moments occur when the state fluctuates and suddenly ceases for no apparent reason. These times bring on periods of intense despair, a fear that one has been forsaken by the Presence. These falls make the path arduous, and to surmount these reversals requires great will. It finally becomes obvious that one must transcend this level or constantly suffer excruciating descents from grace. The glory of ecstasy then has to be relinquished,

as one enters upon the demanding task of transcending duality, until one is beyond all oppositions and their conflicting pulls. But while it's one thing to happily give up the iron restraints of the ego, it's quite another to abandon the golden chains of ecstatic joy—it feels as if one is giving up God, and a new level of fear arises, never before anticipated; this is the final terror of absolute aloneness."

Is this what I have been deeply intuiting? Is this pointing to the inchoate knowing of "there is more?" There is embodying, a "leaving" the bliss state of transcendence. I have a deep sense of Hawkins speaking of something beyond my present state of awareness, even though what he says has merit for where I am right now as well.

In my own case, the fear of nonexistence was formidable, and I drew back from it repeatedly. At the retreat in Mill Valley, when Jan asked us what we are most afraid of, I knew without a shadow of a doubt it was annihilation—which appeared to me to be very different than death. And the night a couple of days after the shift, lying in bed and watching as the "sentry" interfered with a full dissolution—something in me pulled away from a complete letting go. Until India, sitting at the foot of the mountain and watching as I spontaneously dissolved, leaving not a trace of form.

This fear of nonexistence is tied to the dissociated state—a psychological state of being. It is understandable that I, as a human, would confuse this ego state of non-being. In my case, as a result of repeated trauma throughout childhood, I was dissociated from my body, from my experiences, from my feelings, and from any sense of really being in this world. This, experientially, was non-existence! This, experientially, was the mind's questioning my existence.

Every single human being is confronted, at some point, with death and most are fearful. The ego, doing its job, holds on mightily.

And yet, embodied presence is profoundly alive and engaged. The intuitive knowing that I would let go of, not cling to, the transcendent state, appears to have struck fear and confusion in my ego. This showed me how crucial it has been to immerse myself in gentleness and in love. How necessary it has been to softly, with kindness, open my heart, my fists, and my clenched gut.

JUNE 28TH, 2014

Now the night after the horrifying descent I am expecting to be dead tired and sleep fully, but once again find myself awake.

With eyes closed I begin to see the dance of awareness, consciousness as the intermingling happens up close—watching as the ephemeral spirit of all that there is permeates every single life form—in fact watch as this spirit moves into form (people, trees, mountains, streams, animals)—and see people infused with consciousness/awareness. I watch, as some people are widely open and seemingly, completely transparent as the divine dances within the cells of the body. And other folks, who, defended, are dense and even though equally infused with the divine, are thick and seemingly unaware of anything inside, underneath, permeating, all around the thick wall of density. And seeing . . . the ever-present, continuity of spirit dance in and through all the forms we mortals assume are "real" and defining.

I have the sense of God watching itself, awareness knowing itself, delighting in the scene. I have the sense of being, being a particular awareness, in each and every moment. Here is the beaver, the dam—being! Here are the mountain rocks, the clouds dripping on its hillside, being. Here is the choir; faces lifted to the heavens, here are the notes of the songs escaping their lips, being. And in this case, in this middle of the night moment of existence, there is the despair and destruction of feeling disconnected from everything, the pain of being locked behind thick walls, the sorrow of not knowing itself, being, and the evaporation, the gentle and natural evaporation of this illusion into omnipresent love.

JUNE 29TH, 2014

And in this same other stream—all of one fabric—

Several weeks ago I accepted an invitation to sit in meditation with some friends. As I settled into the sweet spaciousness sitting with my eyes closed I "saw" a tree, the dog, the people in the room, the hills, and then zoomed out further and "saw" the forests, the mountains, the cities, and the sky, the vast sky. Then zooming out further I "saw" the globe of the earth floating in the universe. Then I zoomed out further and saw the pulsating, quivering aliveness of the still vastness, all of consciousness and beyond, and watched as it wafted inside, through, and around the universe and the earth. All that is—the living, breathing vastness, moving everything, forming everything.

JULY 7TH, 2014

"Knowing others is wisdom; knowing the self is enlightenment."

LAO TZU

I am seeing and knowing the agony of living as if you/I am separate, separate and alone . . . seeing it from the perspective of unity.

Looking at it through the eyes of consciousness I see, actually I feel, our common human experience. We all, at some level, know we are lost. And the distractions we use are to avoid asking the penetrating and important questions. The never-ending things we attend to, desperately trying to feel all right, feel better, believe we are on top of things. From the earliest age we build walls and defenses, we establish patterns of conditioned responses—whatever it takes to survive in what always appears to be an unpredictable and, at times, unsafe world. It is exhausting. It takes so much effort to keep up the sham, the illusions, the attempts at well-being, the search for love, for "safety." We kid ourselves all the time, disguising our needs for connection, for belonging, for security, for recognition. We are running away from our tenderness, our vulnerability. We are confusing fear and dependency with love. Since I worry about you, I must love you. Since I cannot live without you, I must love you. And from this charade, this sham, and confusion, we perpetuate our fears and create a world of disharmony and insist the enemy is out there or something is wrong with us.

And underneath this, sweetly lurking in the shadows, as close as your breath, is the vastness of pure love, the real thing.

August 8th, 2014

There is an internal powerhouse of energy. It is alive, omnipresent, regardless of any outside circumstance. And there is a felt sense—a body awareness of pain, of rage, and of hatred, as if it needs to be known in the body.

I am allowing the force and fierceness. There is no resistance. And there is an opening to the profound stillness that is all around and through this distortion. A stillness that is completely neutral to the distortion, not impacted at all.

Life and love are distorted by my mind and my body, and this warp is felt. It is allowing me to move through this insane culture and to be more and more effortless in relationships.

It needs to be known in the body.

"Step into the fire of self-discovery. This fire will not burn you. It will only burn what you are not."

Mooji

It needs to be known in the body.

"Realization is not complete unless it is extended across all dimensions of our being."

Aisha Salem

Live in it (pain and confusion) effortlessly.
It needs to be known in the body.
Dream:

I am in bed, under the sheets, with C. I am telling him how we both were so enriched by our time together. He is defended, cautious. I say I am not asking him for anything, simply telling him how I see it. He says I might not realize it but anyone walking into my house will only hear the truth and not many people want that.

SEPTEMBER 1ST, 2014

I was under the impression that when the "me" had awakened I would not experience personal discomforts, like pain, embarrassment, anxiety, and disappointments. I was under the impression that they would be erased. Instead all these feelings are being seen and felt, only from a different perspective, without the lingering identifications, meanings, associations that create suffering, that assembles itself into dense matter. Instead it is more like clouds, coming and going. . . sometimes dark and stormy, but always moving.

There is more and more quietness in my mind, and more rest in my being.

OCTOBER 31ST, 2014

I see two pregnant women and I fall into wonder, pure wonder. It is as if I am seeing pregnancy for the very first time. Life in the now is forever new, forever innocent.

NOVEMBER 6TH, 2014

I am in the park, feeding homeless teens with M. (M., an awakened being, cooks hot food for homeless teens daily). I see what looks like a very large yellow rope, serpentine, on the grass, and, as if in slow motion, realize it is a fat, alive, slowly moving snake, belonging to the young girl sitting beside it. She picks it up and settles it around her neck. I notice I have no fear, in fact, have not reacted at all. I find myself fascinated instead. I am aware of how different this is from what it would have been like to be surprised by this gigantic creature before.

DECEMBER 1ST, 2014

"Redeem everything that is hurt, confused. I am no mistake."

ADYASHANTI

202

The power has gone out in my neighborhood, affecting my home and my office. I am woefully unprepared with no working flashlight, no matches, and no candles. I am jangled, jittery. I am standing outside my office, under an awning. It is raining heavily; I have no umbrella and cannot get a taxi. A man stops and asks me if he can help. I am aware of sending off the vibe of a damsel in distress.

I am so surprised to be in this state.

I get into bed—there is a lot of nighttime activity happening inside—it is intense.

Energy is coursing through my body, from the top of my head. I am aware of increasing degrees of fear in my stomach.

Another night, a few nights later, I am awakened with an intense pain and energy around my heart, my back, and my arms. I feel nauseous.

I feel as if I am going to die, literally, from a heart attack. Should I call 911? I am very frightened. I have never had a panic attack and do not fully recognize it for what it is when it is happening.

Another night I am abruptly awakened in the middle of the night, experiencing pure fear. There is intense body pain. I sob. The cells of my body radiate grief, anger, and hate.

In the open realness of whatever is showing up each moment . . . living inside that moment to moment, there is no expectation, no assumption of anything being different than it is—there is, as a river flowing, sensation following sensation, being noticed, being registered, and sometimes, being felt.

FEBRUARY 6TH, 2015

A lot of nighttime energy . . . feels like voltage, like a poltergeist. A strong pressure. Sometimes it fills my entire body—my limbs, the heart area, the top of my head. Sometimes this is uncomfortable and very active throughout the night. Sometimes it is pleasant. I am aware of being re-arranged, whatever that might mean. It feels like a workout, my body adapting, settling, and adjusting to this energy, this pulsating, empty sweet energy.

I have two dreams:

I am making love with a woman, which generates intense energy. The energy starts in the genitals and is very strong and intense. From there it rolls around, moves around the whole body, and I am aware of not being able to adequately describe the happening.

The Second Dream:

I am on the side of a mountain, standing with another person on my left. In front of me is a man facing me—he is nondescript and not particularly familiar. I think to myself, "should I be afraid?" And feel a wash of kindness. I reach my hand out to him expressing kindness.

He takes my hand and we begin to walk down the mountain and I realize, somewhat spontaneously, that this man has done something terrible.

We get to the bottom of the mountain, a somewhat furrowed cavern. He has killed children, many children (all around the age of two years old) and the floor of the cavern is covered with their blood. It is anguishing. We walk through the blood and out of it.

I still feel kindness and watch as the man comes out into the open with his head up. He has held onto the kindness.

All is known and all is loved.

JUNE 29TH, 2015

I am aware of coming up inside a deep pattern of accommodating. I see the deeply embedded pattern of being dependent, needing badly, in fact, desperately, to have someone to lean on. I will say whatever I need to say or not say, do or not do whatever it takes for the other person to be there.

And here is the depth of it—it lives inside as if I will die if the other person is not there. Die, as a dependent baby who is not fed and sheltered, would die. Die, as a dependent baby, who is not connected to another being, will die.

And when another is not there, sufficiently, I feel terror and grief. When the other is not even aware they are not holding up their end of things, there is rage.

It is liberating to see the pattern. That night it gets clearer as the realization is felt in the body.

Everything needs to be known in the body.

There is a paradox that shows up as wisdom. There are times that it is necessary to pay attention to patterns—to feel, and to know, what is making you react. And there are times it is sufficient to simply notice reactions, feelings, and thoughts as they show up and leave.

When there is a commitment to the truth, what needs to be seen and felt through will stick around—the bigger and denser stuff. It might show up over and over, it might be intense; one way or another, it will announce its presence. Otherwise what is showing up will, effortlessly, move and disappear like the clouds in the sky.

DECEMBER 27TH, 2015

I am lying on the couch, the sun filtering through the window, warming my skin. I am deliciously relaxed, happy to be here. I sit up, watch the world go by outside my window, and then come back to resting on the couch. I am suddenly and fully aware of it being time to retire. The knowing is quiet and clear, on one hand the most natural realization, and on the other, a tremendous surprise. I had assumed I would die in my psychologist's chair, happily listening to people. I love what I do, feel privileged by the intimacy and trust, and could not imagine, other than poor health or death, why I would stop doing this.

And yet, here it is, full clothed, clear as a bell, it is time to stop. To whatever degree I am tied to, showing up as a healer has run its course. The energy for it has dried up. In speaking to a couple of my supervisors about a particular patient, one who is deeply stuck, one bit of advice was the possibility of increasing our times of meeting up to five days a week, in the hope that over a period of many years (like ten) he could and would let go of his thick wall of defenses. Ten years! I would be eighty-two. Is this how I want to spend the last years in this body, on this earth? Apparently not!

* * *

My days are filled with beginning the leaving-process with all my patients. I am aware of a keen consciousness—an attuned sensitivity to how everyone is feeling about this, including me.

Day after day I process with each patient my leaving and the end of our work together. I am aware of how little we human beings, collectively speaking, know how to or are willing to face loss and endings with honesty and integrity, probably because it hurts a great deal.

And my leaving is for my own good—my patients have little to no say in that matter. Our goodbye must include their feelings about that.

I often feel we are doing hospice work. There is a death happening every moment, always, one of us or both of us are aware of our upcoming ending, and depending on what else might be going on that day, we talk about it. There is a relief, a breathtaking opening, whenever someone is able to say it like it is. We review their lives from the perspective of our work together. We speak of what it has been like to know each other. We say our goodbyes, knowing it is likely we will not see each other again once our time together comes to an end.

There is a freedom in not being constrained by the structure and agenda of how to do therapy. Without the distance of therapist/patient I can show up to be with each and every patient in an intimate present. We say I love you to each other frequently and it is heartfelt and real. Knowing we are parting ways, that we are dying to each other, having grown accustomed to knowing we would see each other again, next week or in a couple of days, it is like a deathbed, only the essential remains. We have walked together, closely, and shared secrets and terrors, joys and surprises. In some cases this is the most intimate relationship they have known, the deepest and clearest they have been seen—for better and for worse. And, what we all long for, they are loved, no matter what. In many cases it is vulnerable, and takes courage to feel love and even more so to express it out loud.

I am often in awe at these endings. It is as if the most therapeutic thing we have ever done together is saying goodbye. For many people it brought them to places they could previously only imagine—a self-acceptance, a willingness to feel love, an unguarded,

undefended heart, a facing of reality, absent of illusion or willful-
ness. Being present, no matter what is felt or seen.

There are a lot of tears!

* * *

I am relieved. I have given up my office, shut off the phone and
the lights, hung up my work clothes, given up my professional
license and insurance, ended supervision, and let go of all structure and schedules.

I am grieving.

JUNE 6TH, 2016

I am moving without thought—being aware without thought.

My grandson is going to sleep on the living room sofa and I, very
sleepily, curl under the covers in my bedroom. Without knowing
why, and even though almost asleep, I find myself getting up, walking into the darkened living room, and standing there for a while,
watching my grandson lying on the couch. I walk over to him and
find him wide-awake, frightened by something, and not being able
to sleep. I sit with him; hand on his leg, until he falls asleep.

A friend is spending the night, and once again, even though I
am under the covers and relishing falling asleep, I find myself getting up and knocking on the door to the guest room. My friend is
allergic to a scent on the sheets; we remove them from the bed and
replace them with others that don't have a scent.

EMBODIMENT
JUNE 12TH, 2016

I didn't have adequate words for what I felt called into . . . it is only
in retrospect that I see it is a call to embodiment; an embodiment
of presence—an integration of spaciousness, ease, and neutrality
down to the cells of the body. A holy marriage of the divine and
the human. No separation! No false division! Bringing love into
the flesh.

There is maturing happening:

"The hero gives a wooden sword to his son
Until he learns to use a
real battle sword
Human love is a wooden
Sword
Until he learns to battle
hurt with mercy."

RUMI

I am drawn to body meditation and somatic awareness. I sense this as a helpful tool. I spend forty-five minutes every day with my eyes closed, lying on my bed, listening to a Jon Kabat-Zinn guided journey bringing consciousness to my body, inch by inch. The meditation guides my awareness, slowly and gently, from my toes up to the crown of my head. Day after day, noticing the subtle and sometimes loud pockets of embedded emotions in different parts of my body.

I love it. I mean really love it. It is deeply relaxing—it appears to be aiding a deep letting go in my body. I have intuited for a while now that my body is waking up. After being in a deep freeze of dissociation for decades it is finally getting the message that it is safe enough to thaw, come to life, and "join the party." It is amazing. I'm beginning to fall in love with my body—for real. I weep with gratitude each time I scan it.

I am particularly surprised by the hate and stress I feel in my jaw and face. I would not have expected it to be living there—in my gut maybe, maybe even in the heart. The sensation of hate is intense. I can grit my teeth and feel the strength and energy of hatred. I breathe into and through it, over and over.

JULY 15TH, 2016

This morning's body scan . . . lots and lots of thoughts and distractions. Throughout I feel a fury and sense a growl—an animal's roar . . . a roar against confinement. Certainly there are the all too familiar struggles in this world, adapting, conforming, and restricting ourselves to fit in. This seems like the growl of rage and despair coming from staying small. This howl is the awareness of the human suffering of living within the maddeningly restrictive illusions of the mind and feelings.

The suffering does not come from our illusions per se, it comes from our resistance. Being with the restriction, being with the moments of the limited mind at play is freedom. Life flows in and through everything. I am aware of continuing to learn. And deepen. Now consciousness is freed. It flows, moves, flies. It can live through the body . . . as the body. It can, and does, move through form as form. Hallelujah.

July 30th, 2016

In today's body scan, I am noticing a "rescuer" pattern. How much of my energy has gone into helping others, sensing what they need, and offering it—sometimes out of a desire to care (often a self serving caring), sometimes out of fear, and sometimes out of a desire to control them. This is dropping away. I had a conversation with a friend and I notice that I stayed with how I really felt. I said it truthfully and kindly in a straight-forward way. "I am available these times and not these." I said this without a pretend sweetness, without extra friendliness (to protect myself from her potential reaction). I asked her if she could accommodate my schedule without being attached in any which way. I am aware—in this present interaction—of uncovering vestiges of ego and win/lose thinking. It is either she or I!

I wonder about letting go here . . . in a big way . . . of built-up attachments. It appears to be a bigger deal than I had anticipated. Something seems to be irrationally and fearfully holding on. I am having stomach cramps.

Hear/see/watch everything lovingly, compassionately, including, and maybe especially, my own expressions and responses.

AUGUST 2ND, 2016

Third or fourth bout of stomach cramps. There is a strong pressure throughout my body. A whole lot of body heat . . . my whole body is radiating heat and sweating.

I am up much of the night with cramps. My mind is giving me trouble. There is a bit of fear of being afraid. There are physical discomforts and pain. I am agitated about relationships, especially around not accommodating. My mind is going over it, again and again, as if it could figure it out, find a solution, and feel okay.

I notice the fear, the anxiety, and the resentments, without any resistance. I see it and it evaporates—sooner and sooner. Again, in retrospect, I can see how agitated my mind became in the face of letting go of the deep, deep pattern of dependency and accommodating. A big death!

AUGUST 4TH, 2016

I am with other folks for a week and notice that even though someone is moody and frequently uncommunicative, I have no reaction. It doesn't even seem to occur to me to take it personally—what I am most noticing is how different this is than how I had been before.

And even more impressive is that the spaciousness that is alive inside is wide enough, present enough (quietly, without a word being spoken) to hold the "other" person as well, and in front of my eyes I see his mood dissolve and watch him lighten up, over and over again.

AUGUST 10TH, 2016

I am on a Disney cruise with my family—all the Disney characters are congregated in the main lobby, surrounded by dozens and dozens of children (with parents and cameras close by). The characters and the children are dancing and singing and I am in tears, my heart bursting at the seams, to be in the midst of such innocence and unabashed joy. It is palpable and opens every cell in my body and every pore of my being. I lose all sense of boundaries.

Later, I am in Golden Gate Park feeding dozens and dozens of homeless teens. My friend, M., has been cooking them hot meals and brewing them loose-leaf tea for years and I have joined him for the last year. The experience has been sweet—truly sweet. The kids love my friend and he adores them, calling them his angels. For a year I have been basking in the glow of this love, enjoying eye contact with each and every person we feed, and having intermittent conversations.

This evening, though, the kids are high on a different drug, and even though we are in the midst of a large group of kids, roaming, sitting, and lying down, there is no contact whatsoever. I am aware of pouring them tea, of asking them if they would like a homemade cookie and of an extra grunginess to the scene. I am aware that I feel no fear although strung out teenage boys surround us. I am aware of the moment-to-moment reaching out and walking from one to the other.

It is after I get home, after I settle into the evening that I register the unbearable anguish, the pain, despair, and the utter "lostness" of these kids. It is a pain unlike anything I have experienced, truly intolerable. I registered it all, deeply, and in this moment I feel it all.

Being open, being empty, being transparent does not discriminate. I feel it all—innocence and anguish. And it is all right . . . truly all right. I feel whatever I am feeling, and it moves on.

I walk by the pet hospital on Fillmore Street and notice a woman come out the front door and collapse (standing up) against the wall. I spontaneously look into her eyes, immediately getting that she has put a beloved pet to sleep. I quietly mouth, "I am sorry," as I feel the unfiltered pain and notice myself crying. She nods her head and mouths "thank you." I walk on down the street and the pain leaves, completely gone inside me, replaced by the scent of the air blowing. Emptiness!

SEPTEMBER 12TH, 2016

I am retired. I am reveling in the freedom to "move as the spirit moves." My days and hours are open-ended and I have the spaciousness and leisure to roam. I take the train from Emeryville, California to Brattleboro, Vermont. It is a joy to live on a train for five days and nights, seeing the country from this vantage point. The scenery is magnificent; the Rocky Mountains take my breath away, especially chugging right through them. I am struck by how wonderful it feels to explore and move unimpeded. I have no restrictions, inside or out.

I am living on a mountainside in southern Vermont. I am spending three months in the midst of the fall foliage.

I am living in and from unity—deepening into it, this experience, and knowing everything is God, everything is welcome into His house . . . this body. Being everything . . . the flower, the Black Panther, the wide road . . . a cranky mood. It is all one—one continual oneness.

SEPTEMBER 20TH, 2016

Everything will be known, nothing can be left out—there is no out. It is like an archeological dig—I enter so tender, so open— and find layer upon layer of conditioning having been built up. Dense, dark, covered, blind, lost, and confused layer upon layer. With consciousness, clear eternal awareness, ever present, my goodness, ever present, without any effort and with no beginning or ending, calling forth. Pulling piece after piece of darkness into its orbit of light, into the bounty of love.

I pass by a path to a mountain trail. I have walked by this path dozens of times and didn't recognize it as a path. This time I see the sign . . . and now that I see the sign it looks so blatantly obvious. It is, in fact, hard to miss.

But it hadn't been obvious the many, many times I walked by it previously. Like oneness, our true nature, the realizing of it. So, so obvious when the illusions of our world, the illusions of our small selves are seen through. I am left with the sense of how it is possible that we humans miss it again and again, when it is this nearby and as simple as our breath.

We get so lost in our thoughts, our made-up world, lost in the forest of bewilderment and suffering, convinced of our beliefs, we miss the truth beating in our hearts, showing and opening the path to what we truly are.

These days the path into deeper maturation is through my body. I am doing yoga. I have been moved to yoga in much the same way I began Kabat-Zinn's body meditation. It seems to be another way of entering more fully into my body by moving, bending, balancing, being centered, and becoming physically stronger. I am walking a pathway through the mountain, right outside my studio, my feet, inside my shoes, making contact with the earth, flexing my toes giving me a sense of connectedness and balance. My entire body is open—my heart, eyes, ears, throat, and fingertips—open to whatever shows up. My arms swing along to the sounds of the forest . . . I am rejoicing. What a feeling; what a sensation, what a novelty, to be embodied—to be here in a whole new way. I am no longer dissociated, no, I am fully here, being alive in every cell, muscle, and joint. I am standing rooted in my body, and I feel reborn.

"Moses sees the bush as it actually is . . . all that is living burns. This is the fundamental fact of nature. And Moses saw it with his own two eyes directly. That glimpse of the real world—of the world as it is known to God—is not the world of isolated things but of processes in concert. God tells Moses, 'Take off your shoes, because the ground where you are standing is holy ground.' He is asking Moses to experience in his own body what the burning bush experiences: a living connection between heaven and earth, the life that stretches out like taffy between our father the sun and our mother the earth. If you do not believe, this, take off your shoes and stand in the grass or in the sand or in the dirt."

WILLIAM BRYANT LOGAN

"What is to give light must endure burning."

Viktor Frankl

Rest in Peace
September 23rd, 2016

Coming into being . . . out of denial and dissociation, waking up from a deep sleep.

Into being . . . I am dying into being.

I am finally quiet enough to fully rest. Effort is draining out. It has taken so much effort, enormous, draining effort to guard against pain . . . to resist and fight against reality. It is such simple wisdom to lean into the pain, to lean into reality, whatever is happening right now—shouldn't we be teaching our children this liberating pathway? This trail!

I walk in the woods, falling madly in love with the trees, with the bark, with the varying curves of the branches, with the fern covering the ground, its lusciousness permeating my cells, the woodpecker finding its breakfast, the wasp fiercely guarding its hive, letting me know, in no uncertain terms, to not get any closer.

I sit at the pond, hour upon hour, completely still. The dragon-flies visit, flying closer and closer, landing on my thigh. I am the frog, the acorns, and the bees as they swarm and sing a song of joy, buzzing in and out of the center of the flowers circling the pond.

I name the chipmunk that lives under my tiny, and very low to the ground porch. Monk darts in and out, willing to sit on the porch longer and longer the quieter I am. I fall in love with the great out-of-doors and every small and large creature I come across—after a lifetime of being afraid. The days, months, and years of being timid, having to avoid nature and the teeming world of critters.

On the train from San Francisco to Vermont—five glorious days and nights aboard a sleeper car, the landscape of each state distinct, I woke up one morning, looked out the window and recognized Utah, by the craggy mountains flying by as the train rattled forward. The Rocky Mountains, the acres and acres of corn and soy blanketing the Midwest, the Mississippi, and Hudson

Rivers—it was magnificent. On the last day of the trip, a day trip from New York to Vermont I was sitting looking out the window, daydreaming and excited to be close to my final destination—ready to settle in for the three months I am spending in Vermont.

I heard a voice in my head—clear and unassuming—"You have made good use of this life, of this dimension." (I somehow knew "this dimension" meant this world; the implication being this is a place designed to enable us to wake up.)

It is only in looking back that I see how it could have seemed unusual to hear a voice in my head. At the time though, it was completely natural to have a disembodied voice show up and speak to me—as natural as the grass growing or the trees turning color—intimate and familiar—like knowing my mother's voice and heartbeat in the womb. I was tickled to hear from him/her . . . this someone who is both invisible and intimately familiar.

I have so much more direct access and intimacy to reality: knowing directly—it is so much more alive—vibrantly alive.

Living in our heads, our minds, our thoughts, and our opinions is living through abstraction—it is removed, it is one-dimensional, it is flimsy, and dissatisfying.

SEPTEMBER 26TH, 2016

I am sitting at the pond listening to *Moby Dick*. Jeb McKenna, a spiritual teacher, read and analyzed the classic telling of a man's mad obsessions leading to his death, as Herman Melville's expression of waking up into realization of his true nature. The whale represents the world's illusion, driving us to mad distraction and destruction. McKenna takes notice that Ishmael does not die at the end of the story; sanity and clarity are eternal.

Melville tells Ahab to beware of Ahab. As Ahab's frenzy overpowers him and leads him from one destructive decision to another, putting his life and the lives of his crew in mortal danger, he is told that the real danger is from within. The danger comes from self-destruction, illusion, and madness. *Amen to that*!

I am taken by the scene of miles and miles of whales—wide as the eye can see and deep as well. The whales are circling around and around, seeming to be in a frenzy. Melville takes us into this circling whirl of enormous creatures, bringing the reader into the felt sense of something at once awesome and, in another sense, humbling in its power. Even the biggest ship would not want to be caught up or anywhere close to this magnitude of movement and tumult.

We are brought, through the narrator, into the very center of this activity—getting a closer view of what the miles of whales are circling. It is hundreds of female whales with newborn cubs. The cubs are innocent and curious. Preciously tender, they are swimming freely as they explore the water and each other.

I am reminded of the layers of the human psyche, of the mental, conceptual layers of frenzy, and apparent protection that we use to navigate our lives, desperately attempting to shield our innermost tenderness. Believing in death as an ending, death as destructive. Death as something we need to protect ourselves from.

And in our very center, in the deepest region of our heart we are tender, innocent, and curious. We are the eternal, not needing protection.

And Pip . . . Pip falls overboard and is left humiliated and stranded. As he faces death he sees into God. Sees reality clearly. Sees there is no death. Sees we are eternal. And from then on, his friends and colleagues call Pip mad!

The primitive/limited human mind cannot see clearly into reality. It is not possible. It distorts, it is self-serving, by its very nature. Reality is perceived through the quiet small voice of the innermost heart and mind.

SEPTEMBER 27TH, 2016

Last evening I had a conversation with Jan about Bernadette Roberts. Once again, I am struck by Roberts' experience with the self before and after. She writes, in *The Experience of No-Self,* about a further and deeper dissolution of the self into oneness with God:

"...true self—suddenly disappeared, and without center or circumference there is no self, and no divine. Our subjective life of experience is over—the passage is finished. I had never heard of such a

possibility or happening. Obviously, there is far more to the elusive experience we call self than just the ego. The paradox of our passage is that we really do not know what self or consciousness is, so long as we are living it, or are it. The true nature of self can only be fully disclosed when it is gone, when there is no self."

I intuit, feel a pull into, whatever this appears to mean to me. I tell Jan that I am aware of some buffer, some barrier, some something "in the way." I am aware of both not being in charge of this, and aware of the truth of this.

I woke up very early . . . 5:15 a.m.

And realized . . . I am oneness. I am experiencing/knowing oneness . . . moment to moment.

There is being . . . I, viscerally, in the very cells of the body, know that nothing is separate.

I am living a unitive life . . . a unitive life is living through me.

And always letting go—opening my hands and letting life (and a great love) be the guide, again and again. Each moment comes and goes . . .

I am living the unitive life through further attunement to my body. It is, in some ways, a foreign language that is becoming more familiar and more available. I am attuned and recognizing what my body is sensing and feeling.

A direct attunement not bypassed or overlooked through interpretation. I brought a heavy suitcase, backpack, and my computer on the train, crossing the country. I had to stop and change trains in Chicago and New York. I wasn't able to maneuver all my stuff by myself. As each stop came closer I became aware of what I thought was anxiety, a familiar sensation that I was interpreting as worrisome.

I sat with the sensation and realized, "oh, I need to get help," and anticipate how to get it ahead of time since the stops can be short and hectic. I was attuned to the clear need—interpreting it as anxiety and concern confuses and complicates matters. Reacting in any way complicates matters, eclipses reality.

It is what we do . . . complicate matters by reacting. Being angry, hateful, worried, arrogant, controlling, and acting from a deeply held belief that we are separate, alone, and lacking.

When, in fact, we are deeply connected and when attuned we see and know this clearly as life responds intelligently. We might (most likely will) encounter challenges, hard stuff, and difficulties, and even, perhaps, deep, deep sorrow. Being reality is not about escaping life, it is trusting and allowing the life force to come through our being, our bit of cells, skin, and muscles, our expression of ultimate consciousness.

That night I dream: *I went to Jan's house—she is in the back room on the phone. I walk in quietly to not disturb her. I turn facing the door I just came through and without making contact with Jan I go back out. I am in a room, or a suite, where I am staying with all my stuff (and even stuff added, like a camera and tripod). I am leisurely lying around my place, comfortable. When I realize—oh—wait a minute. I cannot stay here. It is costing me rent . . . all the time I am here, it is costing me. I need to pack up and go back to Jan's. I look around for what, for how much, work or packing, is needed.*

Rent is high for unconsciousness.

*"There will never be any more perfection than there is now.
Nor any more heaven and hell than there is now."*

Walt Whitman

Further Dying
October 3rd, 2016

I am contemplating my own death—physically.

I have been sick since last May. I have had four or five episodes of what right now looks like acid reflux/gerds. (I am reminded of the stomach cramps I had during the body scan period—likely the beginnings of this issue.)

I am watching as the body falls apart—I am being with it in a very real way. I am in pain, very vulnerable. I am physically alone and all right, in a real way. The pain and discomfort needs all my attention. My stomach is distended (think five months pregnant) and I cannot lie down without increasing the pressure and pain. I had read a book on after-cancer nutrition and was eating a lot of tomatoes, lemons, and cayenne pepper. Whoops! Now I could only eat oatmeal, bananas, and salads, and very little.

Once again it is my digestion and gut roaring . . . I remember Adya's comments on how the awakening of the gut can signal the end of the ego, the end of the mind.

The pain is relentless. Since I do not have heartburn I wonder if something other than acid reflux going on. I am taking a lot of Tums and Prilosec, only getting temporary relief. I wonder about cancer.

I lean, fully, into dying. Coincidentally I watch two movies about death—*The Barbarian Invasion*, a film about a very sweet goodbye amongst friends when one of them is passing on, and *Two Weeks*, an honest film showing the last two weeks of a woman dying from cancer. I feel into both scenarios, with no resistance.

I am sitting at the pond, in stillness, when Ramana Maharshi comes to me, as if he is sitting beside me. I am with him, at age sixteen, when he believes he is dying—physically dying right then—I am with him as he fully surrenders and gives over into the great unknown.

I also give over, fully. I am aware of being completely at peace, resting in the all-rightness of this eternal moment. I am this moment. I am home, at rest in every cell. I know this, in the deepest chambers of my heart.

I get seriously ill, (side-effect of Prilosec).

There is only spotty internet connection in my studio and intermittent cell phone coverage so I am aware that it could take quite a while for help to come if I needed it.

I am at peace and I know I need to be checked. I go to urgent care in Brattleboro, thirty minutes by car from my studio. The doctor, who himself, suffers from acid reflux, diagnoses me. He tells me there really is little relief; he lives on an extremely limited diet. He also tells me my skin looks yellow to him, and my internist and oncologist should examine me when I return home. He, too, is wondering about cancer.

I go back to the Airbnb and research cancer on the web and find a match for several symptoms—distended stomach, fatigue, and now yellow skin (if that is true). In bed that night, again, I register a deep alright-ness about dying. I feel at peace. For the first time this is deeply true. I know I will go to my oncologist when I get home. If I do have cancer, I will see how I want to be with it. Where will I live, how will I die? I will clean out all my "stuff." If I do not have cancer I will see how I want to be with that. Will I move to the country? Where will I live? How will I live?

Weeks later (after returning to San Francisco) I get a clean bill of health.

A SHIFT
OCTOBER 7TH, 2016

I am doing yoga daily, continuing to strengthen the core and open my body. I enjoy feeling this strength in the body; I enjoy feeling my feet inside my shoes, feeling my fingers spread wide support my torso as I move into yoga poses. I feel strong as I walk up and down the hills of the forest trail, digging deep inside myself as my body makes contact with the rocks and dirt of the road. I like the sensation of the sheets when I lie down on my bed. I like being a body.

I notice a resistance to feeling fatigue, of not getting enough sleep, of feeling depleted. The resistance feels like a filter, a block. I simply notice.

I attend Jan's satsang. She speaks from vastness. I am silent, still.

OCTOBER 8TH, 2016

I am too fatigued for a walk. It is a full body fatigue. I do yoga and stay quiet all day. I stay in my pajamas.

At Jan's satsang I am transcendent. Now, in full humanity I am washing dishes.

There is a spontaneous insight. There is a coming together of "two"—an integration.

In bed at night: I am aware of holding back. Open wider, wider. Love fully.

My heart is burning for a while—straight line across the chest.

OCTOBER 9TH, 2016

I wake up early: 5:15 a.m.
Aware
"I" am completely transparent
Awareness is in the driver's seat
All movement is love

I lay quiet all morning
I feel this energy "move in."

There is pressure in the cranial crown and the heart

And now, I am profoundly aware in the marrow of being, that the manufactured personality we all assume ourselves to be, who is destined to break, to shatter, and in the shattering, breaking, and dissolving of our illusory self it evaporates, so the movement of our true essence lives our existence, a life of a fully realized being in the marvel of human form. We are not who we think we are! This knowing is fresh each moment, every moment! It is fresh and it is breathtaking, each moment. I want to shout out, again not for the first time: "don't miss out on this marvel!"
There is a filling in . . . being has taken over.

"I see clearly that our humanness and our divinity cannot be two,
and love—the kind of love that survives crucifixion—
is all that really matters."

JEFF FOSTER

I am happy to be alive. I remember, many years ago, walking along a path in nature I had a realization. "You are not really here! You will leave this earth and have not experienced it at all." I recognized the truth of this revelation but could only intuit what in heaven's name that really meant or what was required for that to change.

And now, I am fully and gratefully here. Here to fully experience, here to fully love, and here to bow to all the delights, heartbreaks, and surprises this life has to offer.

Through dying, over and over, I am one.

And I see there is no end. This moment, and every moment, breathes in and out for eternity.

Permissions

Grateful acknowledgment is made to the following for permission to reproduce from published work:

From *Love Poems From God: Twelve Sacred Voices from the East and West* by Daniel Ladinsky, copyright 2002 used with permission.

Excerpt from *The End of your World—Uncensored Straight Talk on the Nature of Enlightenment* by Adyashanti, Sounds True, Inc., 2010 was used with permission from the publisher.

"The Reed Flute's Song" from *The Essential Rumi*, Translations by Coleman Barks with John Moyne, copyright 1995 used with permission.

Excerpts from *Daughter of Fire: A Diary of a Spiritual Training with a Sufi Master* by Irina Tweedie, The Golden Sufi Center, copyright 1986, 2006 used with permission.

Correspondence with Jan Frazier used with permission.

A concerted effort has been made to clear all permissions for this book. If any required acknowledgements have been omitted, it is unintentional. If notified, the publisher will be pleased to rectify any omission in future editions.

Thanks

Writing this book and being immersed in my life from a bird's eye perspective humbles me when it comes to giving thanks. It is a life rich with guidance and help.

In the beginning . . . my parents, my grandparents, my sweet dear aunt Gloria, and uncle Jack. Thank you.

At every turn of my life, especially the low points, I have happened upon a beautiful and wise person. I am eternally grateful to June Singer and Deborah Melman, two women who cared for me, sat with me, and held my hand as I walked through many a dark tunnel.

To Adyashanti, Jan Frazier, David Hawkins, and Mooji—who, through empty presence, shone a light into my essence, and the way home, I bow to what we all know and forget. And to the sparks of lights that continue to refresh our memories and our deepest knowing. Thank you.

To David and Victoria, thank you for your youthful curiosity and for your genuine interest in this book. Our over-coffee conversation warmed my heart.

I had the good fortune of finding Paul Cohen, editor. I had no idea how much better the book could be until he got his hands on it. He cut and cleaned, cleaned and cut, in ways I would not have had the courage or insight to do myself. He strengthened it, he helped my voice become more succinct and clear, and he sharpened the reach of the message. Thank you.

Thank you Colin Rolfe for the lovely interior design and Jill Kramek for your insightful copyediting. I so appreciate the care and attention you both brought to my work.

To my daughter-in-law Eva Prieto, talent extraordinaire, thank you for the beautiful cover design, for the hours of collaboration, and honest conversations to make it just right.

To Rick Miller, thank you for patiently snapping shot after shot to capture the beauty and grandeur of the Grand Canyon as a perfect backdrop for my photo. I admire and cherish your gigantic heart.

To Lynne Ostrander, Louise Smith, Eva Prieto, Hilary Foster, Teresa McGlashen, Loren Eskenazi, and Dona Tversky—thank you for your early readings and loving encouragement. It is an act of love to willingly and happily offer your time to read a friend's (long) book.

Thank you Lara Darrow, Ifeoma Ikenze, and Patricia Meadows for your gifts and talents in healing and attuning. My more grounded and healthy body salutes you.

To Craig and Eva, Rick and Julie, David, Daniel, Joshua, Casey, and Ryan—I feel so fortunate to have you dear, unique, and amazing people as my family. The world is enriched for having each one of you in it.

A gigantic wave of gratitude for life in it's love and intelligence, bumpy ride, and insistence to wake up to what we really are.

About the Author

 Beth Miller, Ph.D., trained as a psychologist and lives in San Francisco. She is the author of *The Woman's Book of Resilience* and has had a gratifying career devoted to helping people discover their innate wholeness. She studied resilience, wondering what allowed people to be able to love no matter what conditions or circumstances they lived in and through.

She taught at California Institute of Integral Studies and The University of San Francisco Medical Center. She had a private practice of psychotherapy for twenty-five years and gave seminars, talks, and workshops on cultivating resilience.

Her deepest devotion, throughout her life has been to the discovery and embodiment of our truest nature. This devotion, through deep psychological inquiry opened her heart and mind— bringing her into the abiding company of kindness.

She experienced a profound shift in consciousness at the age of seventy and is along for the ride of intimate contact (presence) with what life has in store from moment to moment, and day to day.

She treasures watching her five extraordinarily kind grandsons find their way in the world. They bring her enormous joy and belly laughs.

www.bethmillerphd.com

CPSIA information can be obtained
at www.ICGtesting.com
Printed in the USA
LVHW04s0842241018
594370LV00026B/321/P